Charles A. Lindbergh

An American Life

Charles A. Lindbergh

An American Life

Edited by
TOM D. CROUCH
Associate Curator of Astronautics
National Air and Space Museum

with contributions by

WAYNE S. COLE
MICHAEL COLLINS
JOHN GRIERSON
RICHARD P. HALLION
PAUL R. IGNATIUS
DOMINICK A. PISANO
JUDITH SCHIFF

Published by the
NATIONAL AIR AND SPACE MUSEUM
SMITHSONIAN INSTITUTION

Distributed by the
SMITHSONIAN INSTITUTION PRESS

Washington City

1977

Library of Congress Cataloging in Publication Data

Charles A. Lindbergh.

Lectures presented at a symposium commemorating the 50th anniversary of Lindbergh's transatlantic flight; the symposium was held May 20, 1977, and was sponsored by the National Air and Space Museum.

Bibliography.

1. Lindbergh, Charles Augustus, 1902-1974 — Congresses. I. Crouch, Tom D. II. Cole, Wayne S. III. National Air and Space Museum.

TL540.L5C48   629.13′092′4 [B]   77-14537

ISBN 0-87474-342-7

ISBN 0-87474-343-5 pbk.

All photos used in this book are drawn from the Charles A. Lindbergh Collection, Sterling Memorial Library, Yale University. Unless otherwise noted, all photos are credited to Yale University. Page 37 *(above);* Sport and General Press Agency, London; page 66 *(below),* page 67, page 69, Kurt Huhle, Munich; page 99, Daniel Lebee, Paris; page 100 *(below),* Department of Medical Photography, St. Lukes Episcopal Hospital and Childrens Hospital, Houston, Texas; page 104, Harcourt Brace Jovanovich.

Table of Contents

"Some people may ask, but what was the lesson of Lindbergh's first Atlantic flight for the more distant future? The immediate one was that in breaking the world's distance record by flying 3,616 miles in 33½ hours from New York to Paris he had demonstrated in the most striking possible way what the airplane could do. Yet it was still a long way from being able to carry a load of passengers in safety across the Atlantic in all weather. As with all pioneers, Lindbergh gave his *idea* for himself and others to develop and extend in a practical way. The physical work of the pioneer is secondary to his idea. It is his *idea* which counts, backed by his courage in risking his life to prove that his enterprise is the key which will open the door of the future."

JOHN GRIERSON

May 1977

This volume is dedicated to the memory of John Grierson (1909–1977). While delivering the keynote address in this symposium on the evening of 20 May 1977, Mr. Grierson suffered a stroke. He died later that evening at the George Washington University Medical Center.

Acknowledgments

The editor wishes to express his gratitude to the following individuals for their assistance in the preparation of this volume. Michael Collins and Melvin B. Zisfein, director and deputy director of the National Air and Space Museum, conceived of the symposium and assisted in the selection of speakers. Donald Lopez and F. C. Durant III, NASM assistant directors of aeronautics and astronautics, were a constant source of encouragement and assistance. John Whitelaw, NASM executive officer, was instrumental in arranging for the publication of the papers. Special thanks go to Anne Morrow Lindbergh, who kindly allowed access to the Lindbergh photo collection. Judith Schiff, research archivist at Yale University Library, acted as a knowledgeable guide to the collection and arranged for photocopying. Richard Hallion assisted in photo selection and served as general advisor on the preparation of the volume. Catherine Scott, NASM librarian, assisted in the preparation of the bibliography. Felix Lowe, deputy director of the Smithsonian Institution Press, arranged for editing and publication services. Jeannette R. Mueller served as final editor of the manuscript, and Gerry Valerio designed the volume. Leslie Jo Olsen typed the bibliography. Diane Pearson typed the remaining manuscript.

Foreword

MICHAEL COLLINS

When a reporter asked me recently, "Was Lindbergh a hero of yours when you were a boy?" I had to answer honestly that he wasn't. But today, thirty years later, I can answer with equal candor that he is.

We (the crew of Apollo 11) invited Lindbergh to come to our launch from Cape Kennedy. He did, but, unfortunately we were in quarantine and did not get a chance to meet him. My disappointment was assuaged somewhat when I received, shortly after the flight, a long letter from him. Again I was in quarantine, so I had plenty of time to digest it. In it he said, "There is a quality of aloneness that those who have not experienced it cannot know—to be alone and then to return to one's fellow men once more.... As for me, in some ways I felt closer to you in orbit than to your fellow astronauts I watched walking on the surface of the moon." Later I asked him if I could quote his letter in a book I was then writing, I sent him a copy of the manuscript so he could see in what context I would be using it. His reply was a most pleasant surprise: Not only could I use the letter, but he would write a foreword to the book "if I liked."

This was in January 1974, seven months before he died. I'm not sure whether he knew he was ill or not. But, over the next couple of months, as his foreword took shape, we had several phone conversations and exchanged several letters. After each communication, I was more impressed than before. The two qualities I was the most struck with were the thoughtfulness and the humility of the man. He was doing me an extraordinary favor, one that required long and uncompensated hours of his time, yet he acted as if our roles were reversed, as if he were working for me, as if I were bestowing some honor on him. He was most concerned about his deadline because he didn't want to delay the book. He was concerned that I or my publisher would not like the introduction, and he stressed that we were under no obligation to use it. He proofread the book, and suggested valuable changes. For instance, his knowledge of human physiology (learned from Alexis Carrel?) saved me from including a quite inaccurate analogy of the response of the cardiovascular system to weightlessness.

All in all, it was an extraordinary performance and at a time when he obviously was busy with other things. On 11 February he wrote, "I leave Switzerland tomorrow, but will be several more days in Europe — Frankfurt, Paris, etc. Thereafter I expect to fly to New York and Connecticut and then back to Hawaii." But through all this he took the time to do a first-class job and contributed a foreword that patched up some of the deficiencies in the book. I had almost ignored Goddard completely, but Lindbergh took considerable pains to stress his importance and their own early relationship. He also discussed his flight in the *Spirit of St. Louis* in a way I had not considered before: "I had been without sleep for more than two days and two nights, and my awareness seemed to be abandoning my body to expand on stellar scales. There were moments when I seemed so disconnected from the world, my plane, my mind, and heartbeat that they were completely unessential to my new existence. Experiences of that flight combined with those of ensuing life have caused me to value all human accomplishments by their effect on the intangible quality we name 'awareness'."

I like to think that working with Charles Lindbergh briefly in the closing months of his life has made me more aware — aware of how to maintain one's balance and perspective, of how to be humble and thoughtful and helpful to others. Although he was never a hero of mine when I was a kid, he is now, and therefore this symposium is of special importance to me. The publication that Dr. Crouch has assembled will present his remarkable achievements from many different vantage points. Each contributor is an expert in his field, and I am delighted that they have all agreed to set their thoughts to paper, to bring together the many disparate aspects of Charles Lindbergh's life into one coherent whole.

MICHAEL COLLINS graduated from St. Albans School in Washington, D.C., and received a bachelor of science degree from the United States Military Academy in 1952. He completed the advanced management program at Harvard Business School in 1974. He holds honorary degrees from Stonehill College, St. Michael's College, Northeastern University, and Southeastern University.

Michael Collins spent twelve years as an Air Force pilot before joining NASA as an astronaut in 1964. In his first mission he piloted the three-day Gemini 10, and he became America's third man to walk in space. Michael Collins's second flight was on Apollo 11, launched 16 July 1969. He remained in orbit while Neil Armstrong made his "giant leap for mankind." He has logged eleven days in space and approximately 5,000 hours in a wide variety of aircraft.

He is a major general in the Air Force Reserve.

In January 1970, Michael Collins left the space program to accept an appointment as Assistant Secretary of State for Public Affairs. On 12 April 1971, he was appointed to his present position as director of the National Air and Space Museum.

In 1974, he wrote *Carrying the Fire,* describing his experiences in the space program, and for a younger audience interested in space, his *Flying to the Moon and Other Strange Places* was published in 1976.

Introduction

TOM D. CROUCH

F
ew events in the history of aviation have so electrified the nation and the world as did Charles A. Lindbergh's solo transatlantic flight of 1927.

On the most obvious level, the flight was a demonstration of the maturity of aeronautical technology, forecasting the day when scheduled transatlantic air service would become a reality. However, it was the public perception of the Lindbergh personality that was to lend symbolic significance to the event. Jazz-Age Americans refused to view the flight as a simple triumph of technology over time and space. Rather, Lindbergh's achievement was seen as a reaffirmation of the importance of traditional values that seemed increasingly vulnerable in a more and more complex and mechanized world.

Charles Lindbergh could hardly have chosen a more auspicious moment to make his appearance on the American scene. The twenties had been a decade in search of a hero. Unlike other celebrities of the period, Lindbergh performed, not within the artificial restrictions of the playing field or on the movie lot, but on the limitless stage of the sky. Other pilots seeking to capture the $25,000 Orteig Prize had adopted a team approach. Many had chosen to fly large multiengine aircraft that seemed to offer some measure of safety and comfort. Charles Nungesser, François Coli, Noel Davis, Stanton Wooster, Richard Byrd, René Fonck, and Clarence Chamberlain had all tried and failed. Stories of the death and injury of would-be transatlantic aviators had filled newspaper headlines for weeks.

Lindbergh appeared suddenly, setting crosscountry speed records as he flew from San Diego to Saint Louis, then on to New York. His airplane, a small single-engine monoplane, had been constructed by a relatively unknown firm in only sixty days.

Lindbergh dared to begin his journey while others waited for a break in the foul weather over the North Atlantic. The take-off, a series of bounces off muddy Roosevelt Field, seemed calculated to impress spectators with the dangers inherent in the enterprise. Then he was gone, flying alone while a world waited in suspense. From the moment the *Spirit of St. Louis* touched down at Le Bourget, the millions who searched for ideals and stability in an age of confusion and anxiety adopted Lindbergh as their own.

Writing in *Popular Aviation* in 1928, aviatrix Margery Brown focused on Lindbergh as the personification of traditional virtues in explaining the wave of enthusiasm and adulation that followed the flight.

> *Lindbergh is a symbol, more or less. It isn't Lindbergh the person who inspires them so much as it is Lindbergh as an ideal. They recognize in him qualities they would like to possess — courage, quiet confidence, modesty, and spiritual freedom.* [1]

The young aviator was cited as an example of the success that would come to those who attacked their problems with courage, confidence, and perseverance. The eighteen-year-old editor of the San Marcos College student newspaper, Lyndon Baines Johnson, was one of many who saw Lindbergh as the ideal role model for young Americans.

> *Lucky Lindy is the hero of the hour, yet the adjective which most characteristically describes Lindbergh is not lucky, but plucky. . . . A sketch of his life reveals the grit and determination that have been outstanding traits of his. . . . He is a simple, straight-forward, plucky lad whose first lesson learned was self mastery. He did not give up when hardship and trials beset him. . . . His pluck carried him through to success and fame. . . . It is a wonderful thing to make the first transocean flight and achieve spiritual independence. Still more wonderful is the fact that this feat lies within the grasp of all of us. Students, the choice lies with you. Do not sigh for Lindbergh's wonderful luck, but determine to emulate Lindy's glorious pluck.* [2]

Charles A. Lindbergh became a folk hero. Catapulted to sudden fame, he was to remain a major public figure until his death in 1974. His continued work in aeronautics helped shape the growth of that industry. His enormous popularity and knowledge of military affairs led to his rise as an influential commentator on domestic and foreign issues prior to 1941. During World War II, Lindbergh aided the development of military aircraft and worked to improve their performance

1. Margery Brown, "What Aviation Means to Women," *Popular Aviation* 3 (September 1928): 52.
2. Lyndon B. Johnson, *College Star* editorial, 5 October 1927, in: Doris Kearns, *Lyndon Johnson and the American Dream* (New York: Harper & Row, 1976), p. 63.

on combat missions. With the coming of peace, he turned his attention to problems of central concern to the citizens of a world beset by environmental problems.

The five lectures that appear in this volume were originally presented at the National Air and Space Museum on the evening of 20 May 1976. We offer them in this more permanent form, together with notes and appropriate collateral materials, not only as a commemoration of the fiftieth anniversary of a great event in the history of American aviation, but as a contribution toward a more complete understanding of the achievements of a great airman.

Tom D. Crouch, associate curator of astronautics with the National Air and Space Museum, is a native of Dayton, Ohio. He received his Ph.D. in history from Ohio State University in 1976. He is the author of *The Giant Leap: A Chronology of Ohio Aerospace Events and Personalities, 1815–1969* and has published a number of other articles on aspects of aerospace history. Dr. Crouch is the 1976 recipient of the History Manuscript Award of the American Institute of Aeronautics and Astronautics. He serves on the history committees of both the American Institute of Aeronautics and Astronautics and the American Astronautical Society.

Charles A. Lindbergh

An American Life

Charles A. Lindbergh

JOHN GRIERSON

The name of Charles Lindbergh is securely notched in history as one of the most famous aviators of all time, equal in eminence to Professor Langley and to the Wright brothers. Lindbergh represents everything that is best in the great and glorious pioneering tradition of the American people.

Charles Augustus was born of a second-generation Swedish father and an Anglo-Scot-Irish mother on 4 February 1902 in Detroit and reared on a small farm in Little Falls, Minnesota. He was an unenthusiastic scholar but had such a mechanical bent that he drove and maintained his father's Model T Ford at the age of eleven. At the same time he loved country life and successfully ran the farm alone for two years from the age of sixteen. At eighteen he embarked on an engineering course at the University of Wisconsin but after two years threw it over to follow his new passion for flying.

After some flying instruction in Lincoln, Nebraska, he started barnstorming as a wing-walker and parachutist and then sent himself solo in the Jenny he had bought at Americus, Georgia, in April 1923. He joined forces with his great friend Bud Gurney who wrote, "We flew plane to plane changes where I picked a wing-walker off Slim's upper wing by flying my wing-tip into the wing-walker's hands."

As a cadet in the Army Air Service Reserve, Lindbergh took his wings in March 1925, having already made his first escape by parachute, the result of a mid-air collision. In June, while testing a commercial airplane called a "plywood special," his craft refused to come out of a spin, and he had to make his second emergency jump from 350 feet. His aircraft narrowly missed him on the way down, and he dislocated his shoulder on landing in a high wind.

In April 1926, he initiated the airmail service between Saint Louis and Chicago as chief pilot of the Robertson Aircraft Corporation in a DH4. Mail flying was extremely tough, and involved landing at night in crude fields, and when the weather became impossible or the fuel ran out, the Irving parachute was there to be used. In his first emergency drop as a result of night fog, he was once again chased by his spiralling airplane. The next jump was also at night but in a snow storm, and he landed relatively normally on top of a barbed-wire fence.

Lindbergh became fascinated by the idea of publicly demonstrating how the airplane could connect the New World with the Old. He did not think Atlantic weather could possibly be more dangerous than the weather he had encountered on the night mail. With nearly 2,000 pilot hours behind him, he felt he only needed a proper airplane and he'd be off.

With the backing of nine Saint Louis businessmen, Lindbergh ordered a special airplane, which was to be built in two months by the Ryan Airlines. His new craft was a high-wing monoplane offering the pilot, sitting behind an enormous fuel tank, no forward view. It was powered by a 220 hp Wright Whirlwind J5C 9-cylinder radial, which had a reputation for great reliability.

He planned the flight meticulously. Radio was out because of weight and unreliability, as was a sextant, because he thought it would be impossible to hold an absolutely steady course and take sights simultaneously. He would rely entirely on dead-reckoning and hoped to be able to obtain sufficient sightings of the ocean to calculate windspeed and direction from the waves. He expected a tailwind on his 3,614-mile flight and to average 100 mph: tankage for 4,210 miles in still air should give an adequate margin. He divided the great circle route from New York to Paris into 100-mile sectors and planned to alter course every hour to take into account the curving track and changes of magnetic variation. His navigational instruments included an ordinary magnetic compass, an earth inductor compass, a turn and slip gyro, and a drift sight (which he never used).

Having concluded all tests by early May 1927, Lindbergh flew his machine, now christened the *Spirit of St. Louis,* from San Diego to Saint Louis. The engine almost stopped at night over the foothills of the Rockies because of carburetor icing, and as soon as he reached Curtiss Field in New York he had a heater fitted.

On 19 May, the mid-day Atlantic weather prospects for the next day were grim, and he decided to cancel. When Lindbergh made a final check that evening, an unexpected change for the better was reported, and he reversed his plans and arranged to have his airplane ready at dawn. On reaching the aerodrome after a sleepless night, he was relieved to find no signs of activity on the part of his Atlantic rivals, Byrd and Chamberlain.

Charles as an only son was doted on by his mother who had even accompanied him to college to protect him from girls. She naturally came to New York to see him before the flight.

Lindbergh had earlier ordered the *Spirit of St. Louis* towed to Roosevelt Field where Byrd had sportingly given him permission to use his 5,000-foot special grass runway.

The tanks were filled to 450 gallons. Lindbergh knew that failure to take off would mean almost certain death in a blazing inferno.

That morning the ground was soggy, the clouds low with light and variable wind, and fine rain was falling as Lindbergh started his take-off attempt. When he waved the chocks away and opened the engine up to full throttle, the airplane hardly moved because of the mud and the overload. The spectators ran forward and heaved on the struts until the *Spirit of St. Louis* was going faster than they could run.

Lindbergh cleared the telephone wires by about 20 feet. The pilot had triumphed over the first and one of the greatest obstacles of his flight, and he made his way above Long Island at 200 feet. Presently the rain stopped, the mist and clouds eased, and a tailwind was blowing. Fortune smiled radiantly on the start of his historic flight.

Passing Cape Cod, Lindbergh set out on the first major sea crossing of his life, to Nova Scotia, 250 miles away. He flew at between 20 and 100 feet above the waves, hoping to obtain an advantage by keeping in the ground effect. After only three hours he began to feel cramped and tired and had his first sip of water. In his still-overloaded state, Lindbergh worried about the flexing of the wings, and wondered how long they would stand up to this violent treatment. He reduced his speed as the turbulence built and squall after squall struck. Lightning lit up the trees and rocks of Nova Scotia. For nearly an hour the storm raged until at last the wind went round to the southwest, and he knew the worst was over.

Over the Atlantic again, he found the urge to sleep almost overwhelming. "My eyes feel hard and dry as stones," he wrote. "If I could throw myself down on a bed I'd be asleep in an instant." Then, after shaking his head and body roughly, flexing the muscles of his arms and legs, and stamping his feet on the floorboards, he went on, "The worst part about fighting sleep is that the harder you fight, the more you strengthen your enemy, and the more you weaken your resistance to him." Paris was still 2,800 miles away, and he had a whole night to fly through.

A sudden change in the ocean from open water to a dazzling icefield hit Lindbergh like a bucket of cold water — a stimulant which, added to the instability of his airplane and vibration of the engine, helped to keep him awake.

The ice changed to open water, and he reached Saint Johns 11¾ hours out from New York.

A sense of exhilaration filled the lone flyer as he pointed the *Spirit of St. Louis* out over the mighty Atlantic, heading into the gathering dusk. From the waves he gauged the wind at 30 kt. on his tail. In the fading light, scattered icebergs loomed like eerie monsters, glistening in their dazzling whiteness. Fog lay low on the water, and at first the icebergs showed through, but the fog built up into a solid mass so that Lindbergh had to climb to keep above it. After two hours he was at 9,300 feet.

In the darkness—for there was no moon as yet—he reflected that the going had been almost too easy so far.

As he gazed at the myriad stars, his thoughts turned to religion, to the infinite magnitude of the universe, and to the utter insignificance of man.

Then as he flashed his torch he saw ice beginning to form on the struts and wings, forcing him to turn about. He came out of one cloud pillar and started to weave his path between others, but it was difficult to see their exact shape because the haze made them seem to merge into each other. New York lay fourteen hours behind, yet he felt so worried about negotiating such an array of ice-forming clouds that he seriously considered turning back. The thought was more than he could bear, and he determined to carry on. Miraculously, the ice coating on the wings began to diminish. Although he had lost no height, his two compasses were behaving oddly, making him think he was in a magnetic storm. In the midst of all these worries he began to feel again the irresistible urge to sleep. Luckily, after two hours of solid darkness, the moon started to rise and provide a distraction. The clouds began to look less hostile. Yet, far ahead, moonlight revealed a higher cloud formation that seemed to block completely the way east. Once again the question of turning back throbbed through Lindbergh's mind, and once more he rejected it.

Navigation had suffered from all the alterations of course due to the cloudiness, and from the peculiar behavior of the compasses. On top of that, Lindbergh knew he had been forced 90 miles south of the great circle by the weather to Saint Johns. His drowsiness was affecting his usual aim for perfection, and he felt it would be enough to hit Europe anywhere. As he diverted the slipstream onto his face he wrote: "I let my eyelids fall shut for five seconds; then raise them against tons of weight. Protesting, they won't open wide until I force them with my thumb, and lift the muscles of my forehead to help keep them in place." The *Spirit of St. Louis* refused to be left unattended for five seconds — such was her instability.

Having flown for over five hours out of sight of the surface, Lindbergh was agitated about where the upper winds might have carried him.

Six hours out of Saint Johns brought the dawn. He recorded that " ... the uncontrollable desire to sleep falls over me in quilted layers.... This is the hour I've been dreading; the hour against which I've tried to steel myself. I know it's the beginning of my greatest test—the third morning since I slept." In trying to shake himself into wakefulness, he kept reciting, "There's no alternative but death and failure: no alternative but death and failure." As full daylight came, the urge to sleep lessened slightly, and he was able to keep a better course, refreshed by a sip of water.

At the nineteenth hour, clouds still covered the sea and presented a solid wall ahead, which demanded concentration on instruments. Luckily the earth inductor compass had regained its sanity; but he knew that if he failed to keep the instruments in balance, loss of control and disaster would swiftly follow.

At the beginning of his twentieth hour since New York, Lindbergh began to descend, since he had been unable to see the waves for a wind check for over seven hours. With no knowledge of any change in the barometric pressure, he could not rely on his altimeter reading as he went down, so he decided to limit his descent to 1,000 feet indicated.

Suddenly at 8,000 feet, he saw a deep funnel between pillars of clouds with a heavy sea running on the ocean at the bottom. Anxious not to lose contact, he forced the *Spirit of St. Louis* down until she was diving at 140 mph with the engine throttled back. He had to spiral around the funnel so as not to lose it, descending at such a rate that his ears began to pop. At 2,000 feet, he was under the lowest cloud layer, having lost his sense of direction, but when he had regained his course, he saw he had a quartering tailwind from northwest.

Now he went down to 50 feet above the huge breaking waves and reckoned that the windspeed was up to 60 mph, for the spray was being blown off the white caps like rain. He did not fancy his chances of a forced landing in such a sea, dinghy or no dinghy. His greatest worries were the navigational errors that might have occurred when he had had to alter course so often to avoid the weather with no idea where the wind was carrying him from hour to hour. He felt he might be so far south that he was in danger of striking the Bay of Biscay, yet there were no facts to back his supposition. Before he could decide what to do, fog covered the sea, forcing him to climb, as he was pitched and bucked all over the sky.

After nearly an hour the nose went down without warning, and one wing dropped as he dived towards the waves. Lindbergh had, in his own words, "been asleep with open eyes." Quickly coming to his senses, he applied stick and rudder, intending to correct the dive and get back into level flight. But the turn indicator pointer went hard to port and the airspeed dropped, indicating a steep climbing turn away from where he had just been diving. He was beginning to lose control. The impact of this knowledge acted like an electric shock, and he started to set the instruments into place slowly and deliberately. He did regain a level course, though he felt as if flying in a dream and his conscious mind had ceased to work.

Lindbergh dived right down to within five feet of the waves and, finding himself still in fog, climbed up to 1,000 feet. But in a few minutes breaks started to open up, accompanied by rain. Before a real clearance had arrived, he became aware of ghostly presences in his fuselage, as though a host of vaguely outlined forms with friendly human voices had come aboard. This extraordinary phenomenon did not seem to worry him, though he confessed, "I'm on the border line of life and a greater realm beyond, as though caught in the field of gravitation between two planets, acted on by forces I cannot control. Death no longer seems the final end it used to be but rather the entrance to a new and free existence which includes all space, all time."

Not until the end of the twenty-first hour was the main storm area passed, (though the fringe effects lasted another half hour) when Lindbergh was faced with a new kind of phenomenon — a coastline with hills and clumps of trees in mid-Atlantic. This made him wonder whether he was fast asleep, had flown north to Greenland, or become completely disoriented. How could there be land in mid-Atlantic? An island lay straight across his course, but just as he reached it the shades of grey and white and purple disappeared. The mirage was over, and now the horizon became bright and sharp. He wrote: "I'm capable only of holding my plane aloft and laxly pointed towards a heading I set some hours ago. No extra energy remains. I'm as strengthless as the vapour limbs of the spirits to whom I listen."

He even struck his face sharply with his fist a couple of times as hard as he could and felt no pain to stimulate his body. How on earth could he keep himself awake? "The alternative is death and failure, death and failure," he muttered, and for the first time Lindbergh doubted his ability to endure. He tried every kind of exercise possible in the cockpit and turned his face into the slipstream in a final effort to stay awake. Gradually his strength came back. "I've been hanging over the chasm of eternity holding on to the ledge with my fingertips, but now I'm gaining strength. I'm crawling upwards: consciousness is coming back."

Suddenly a black speck caught Lindbergh's eye, and excitedly he realized that it was a small boat. Sweeping past into a turn he came back low alongside, closed his throttle and shouted at the top of his voice, "Which way is Ireland?" but on his return there was not the slightest response, so he gave it up as a bad job, not wanting to waste any more flying time.

At the turn of the twenty-eighth hour he was flying at 100 feet and scanning the horizon ever more hopefully through breaks in the squalls. He was only half-believing when, on the far horizon between two squalls, he saw a purplish blue band hardened in the haze. Having previously been so misled by a mirage, he was not going to be easily taken in again. If this was Ireland, sixteen hours out from Saint Johns, he'd be two-and-a-half hours ahead of schedule. Still, the wind could easily have done that to him, and this sudden hope brought back full wakefulness. Responding to the temptation, he turned sharply towards the nearest point of what he though was land and, hardly able to believe it, watched a coast of rugged shores and rolling mountains beyond unfold before his eyes. Yes, it really was land. Here was a fiorded coast with barren islands, and from 2,000 feet, he could discern an outline that placed him without doubt at Valentia Island in Dingle Bay on Ireland's west coast, barely three miles from his intended landfall. What a relief, and what a magnificent achievement! One would not think an error of three miles too bad on the twenty-mile crossing of the English Channel, but here, after 1,887 miles through all kinds of weather, Lindbergh had hit Ireland with such a minuscule error.

In acknowledging the wonders of white foam on black rocks, of curving hills, the hospitality of little houses, and the welcome of waving arms, Lindbergh wrote: "During my entire life I've accepted these gifts of God to men, and not known what was mine until this moment. It's like rain after drought, spring after a northern winter. I've been to eternity and back. I know how the dead would feel to live again."

Now it seemed so utterly easy to fly to Paris and land in the dark in six hours time, so long as the weather held. After concentrating on the charts and his onward route, Lindbergh was amazed to look out and see nothing but ocean ahead until he realized that in his excitement he had turned the machine completely round. He soon put that right and delighted in flying low over the Irish farmland with its small houses and grazing sheep. Gone was the wish to sleep, and a new surge of vigor filled his being. All the strain of the ocean had vanished, and now the weather too was improving.

Three hours out from Valentia he crossed Cornwall just south of Plymouth, where the *Mayflower* and so many of his ancestors had originated. Thence over a little more water to traverse the Cap de la Hague near Cherbourg, he flew to Deauville and crossed the main French coast in the afterglow of sunset. This was the moment Lindbergh chose for his first "meal," consisting of a single very unfresh meat sandwich, which he described as tasting rather flat. "Bread and meat," he wrote, "never touched my tongue like this before."

From 2,000 feet, he easily picked out the Seine in the gathering darkness, and he climbed to 4,000 feet in order to be sure of seeing the glow of Paris. There was the Eiffel Tower; he circled it before flying northeast to Le Bourget. He was not sure how far out it was and headed that way, searching vainly for a locator beacon. Eventually, he returned and spotted a concrete apron with airplanes on it.

On slowing down, he noticed how strange the controls of the *Spirit of St. Louis* felt. He realized he must avoid stalling at all costs, but his movements seemed strangely uncoordinated. For the final run he came in fast, aiming just short of some floodlights but overshooting them considerably and sensing that he was about to stall in spite of his speed. There was still plenty of feel left in the controls. He bounced once by the lights, then again as the *Spirit of St. Louis* was enveloped in darkess. That he finished off without coming to any harm, exhausted as he was on this, the first night landing he had ever made in such a blind airplane, and at a strange aerodome, was nothing short of a miracle. Then, on turning to taxi in, he encountered a seething mass of Parisians running to welcome him.

In a darkened hangar, Lindbergh was hidden by two French aviators and the Belgian Baron Willy Coppens. I am indebted to Fred Durant for the following story, which indicates how little Lindbergh appreciated the impact of his flight. After first expressing anxiety because he had no French visa, he produced a scruffy piece of paper and, thrusting it towards Coppens, asked, "Do you know this Paris hotel; I understand it's quite reasonable?"

Why was this solo flight such an astonishing success? Above all, Lindbergh had demonstrated to the world the impact of the airplane's range on transocean communications by flying 3,614 miles from New York to Paris in 33 hours, 30 minutes, 29.9 seconds (FAI official time), at an average of 107.90 mph, incidentally breaking the world's long-distance record. He had won the $25,000 Orteig Prize for the first nonstop flight between New York and Paris. In the last letter I wrote to Charles, I remarked that his Paris flight of 57½ hours without sleep would always stand out as the high-water mark of human endurance in solo flying. He replied with his characteristic and entirely genuine modesty that the significance of his flight lay in being the first link between the mainland of America and the mainland of Europe; the fact that he flew solo was simply a matter of convenience and economy. He brushed aside completely the elements of courage and determination in going on after reaching the safety of Ireland to land in the dark at an unknown Paris aerodrome.

The London crowd at Croydon was even less controlled than the one at Paris, and the first attempt to land had to be abandoned, such was the popular enthusiasm. The maneuvers of welcoming aircraft were somewhat alarming.

At first a destroyer was coming to bring Lindbergh home, which he thought would be rather fun; he was quite disappointed when the cruiser *Memphis* turned up instead.

The welcome home started with forty airplanes, two blimps, and various destroyers in Chesapeake Bay. When the *Memphis* docked, the first person to be ushered aboard was Lindbergh's mother.

At the Washington Monument, President Coolidge received Lindbergh and bestowed the Distinguished Flying Cross on him, the first time it had ever been conferred.

In New York, Lindbergh arrived in a Loening amphibian to a most terrific reception. Everything that would float had been put in the Bay to meet him.

As a nation, the Americans have never been reluctant to show their feelings quite openly as they demonstrated very clearly to the discomfort of the British some years ago at Boston. Now the individual American felt that he personally was involved in the achievement of his national hero and wanted to show in the most unmistakable way his absolute delight in Lindbergh's transatlantic solo pioneering marathon.

At the Battery the fire hoses were playing, and then on Lower Broadway the most fantastic paper snow storm began. Everywhere from open windows tickertape and sheets of paper cascaded in such profusion that the sky was darkened. Never before in history had a man received such a spontaneous and widespread demonstration of welcome.

After one week of such unprecedented celebrations in New York, Lindbergh went to Saint Louis to thank his backers. He saw himself not so much a pioneer as a torchbearer bringing the message of aviation to the people of America. It was for him, having demonstrated with the *Spirit of St. Louis* what the airplane could do, to exhort the public to provide municipal aerodomes and support air services. In fact, his epoch-making flight served as a catalyst of world opinion and inspired a great surge of optimism in support of developing civil aircraft and civil airlines everywhere.

Under the sponsorship of Harry F. Guggenheim, Lindbergh now planned a monster tour of the United States in order to encourage aviation on a nation-wide basis. This circuit (solo in the *Spirit of St. Louis* of course) included sixty-eight overnight stops and a three-month tour of over 22,000 miles beginning on 20 July. He completed the tour almost entirely on schedule and without mishap, thus concluding his second great flight for 1927.

President Callas of Mexico then invited Lindbergh to make an official visit; the young pilot responded on 13 December by flying nonstop through the night to reach Mexico City in twenty-seven and one-quarter hours. On staying with U.S. Ambassador Dwight Morrow, Charles met for the first time the girl who was destined to play such an overwhelmingly active and significant supporting role in his future life.

From Mexico, he continued on an 8,400-mile goodwill tour around the Caribbean, to Saint Louis and thence back to Washington, D.C., where he delivered the *Spirit of St. Louis* to the Smithsonian Institution on 30 April 1928. With his third great solo flight, Lindbergh concluded the flying life of his world-famous airplane.

Lindbergh's New York–Paris flight had been such a dazzling and well-timed event of such worldwide importance, that his last two achievements in the *Spirit of St. Louis* had less impact upon the public imagination. But it should never be forgotten that these tours, totalling 22,000 and 10,500 miles respectively, involved the highest level of the barnstormer's art in getting into and out of diminutive and unknown fields. They constitute a most valuable contribution in exploring future air routes both within the United States and beyond.

JOHN GRIERSON, born 2 January 1909, was educated at Charterhouse and at the Royal Air Force College, Cranwell. Commissioned in 1930, he flew a De Havilland Moth from England to India to join his squadron, making the return trip in 1931 in the record time of 4 days, 10 hours, and 50 minutes. He spent the early years of the thirties in a series of daring distance and endurance flights in light airplanes. These included the *Morning Post* Race, a 9,000-mile flight to Samarkand in 1932, and experimental flights across the Atlantic and around Europe in 1933 and 1934. His solo London-Ottawa flight in a Fox Moth floatplane in 1934 was the first solo crossing of the Greenland ice cap.

It was during this pioneer period of Arctic flying that John Grierson first met Charles and Anne Lindbergh. Grierson's account of his unorthodox introduction to the world-famous flyer offers insight into the character of Charles Lindbergh.

"In 1933 when I had flown to Iceland in my Gypsy Moth seaplane and heard the Lindberghs were coming in from Greenland, I sent a wire to Charles in Angmagssalik saying that I should be glad to meet him and assist in mooring his plane if he would tell me when he expected to arrive. Since he did not answer, and I did not know when he would make his next move, I felt a bit piqued and thought, 'All right, he can make his own arrangements as he evidently does not want my help.' Consequently at the moment the *Tingmissartoq* came overhead, I was busy working in my hangar while the Icelandic reception committee had assembled at the harbor, 3 miles away.

"However, the sea was so rough by the harbor, Lindbergh decided to land in the shelter of my hangar so I ran out and commandeered a ferry-boat in order to take him in tow to a mooring. As you may know, one of the infuriating habits of the British is that they usually forget to introduce themselves which I proceeded to do, so that Charles had no idea I was a seaplane pilot too, and shouted, 'Look out for the pontoons: they're like paper,' as if I did not know that, from my much more fragile little machine!

"In the boat, no formal introductions were necessary and by the time we reached the shore, Charles and Anne had both agreed to visit my hangar for a chat and look at my machine. They not only came later and compared notes — I being particularly struck by how much Anne obviously knew about her radio and used technical words beyond my vocabulary — and Charles, very kindly presented me with the pair of special sunglasses he had used for flying across Greenland so as to protect me from snow-blindness. We were all staying at the hotel Borg and often had meals together.

"At breakfast I found the Lindberghs very sympathetic and Charles immediately arranged to send his mechanics over from his base ship to help me with the work of salvage. [Grierson had damaged his own aircraft in a take-off attempt.]

"It was only after his death that I learned from Anne how worried Charles had been about me in Iceland. Because he thought I was sticking my neck out too far in my little 85 hp De Havilland Gypsy Moth which, coming from him of all people, was no mean compliment.

"What happened in Reykjavik is proof, through Charles Lindbergh's friendly and generous dealings with a complete stranger, of the kind of 'Lone Eagle' he really was."

Before World War II, Grierson served as chief pilot for an airline connecting Portsmouth, Hampshire, and the Isle of Wight, and as operations officer in the Directorate of Operational

14

Services and Intelligence of the Air Ministry. In 1938 he accepted a post as test pilot with Hawker Aircraft and played a major role in testing the first Allied jet airplane, the Gloster-Whittle E. 28/39. During the years following World War II, he was involved in a wide variety of aviation activities, ranging from directing the first serious attempt to use aircraft in conjunction with the Antarctic whaling fleet, to serving as the deputy director of civil aviation in Germany during the Berlin Airlift. After 1950 he worked with De Havilland and Hawker Siddeley in various executive capacities.

Grierson was a member of the Geographical Club and a fellow of the Royal Geographical Society. He served as a member of the R.G.S. Council from 1963 to 1965 and was the United Kingdom representative to the American Antarctic Expedition, Operation Deep Freeze, in 1966. He was the author of *Challenge to the Poles: Highlights of Arctic and Antarctic Aviation* (Hamden, Conn., 1964); *Through Russia by Air* (London, 1934); *Jet Flight* (London, 1946); *Air Whaler* (London, 1949); and a number of other books on polar aviation and on his own flying career. At the time of his death, Grierson had completed *I Remember Lindbergh* to be published this fall.

John Grierson suffered a stroke at the conclusion of his keynote address at the National Air and Space Museum's Lindbergh symposium on the evening of 20 May 1977. He died later that evening at the George Washington University Medical Center.

Charles A., Lindbergh, *The Spirit of St. Louis* (New York: Charles Scribner's Sons, 1953), and the author's personal conversations and correspondence with Lindbergh were the principal sources of material for this paper.

Every Flight for a Purpose

PAUL R. IGNATIUS

I have been asked to reflect on Lindbergh's contributions to commercial air transportation. These were, in my view, the most sustained, profound, and pervasive of all his contributions. The nation's airlines owe much to his vision and his realism.

In the words of the noted airline historian, R. E. G. Davies: "Every flight which Lindbergh made was for a purpose and that purpose was usually the furtherance of airline planning or technical improvement." Restlessly, as an experimental pilot and explorer, he moved beyond individual heroism and personal achievement, which we commemorate today, to help conceive and build the enterprising and enduring airline-aerospace team that has created and maintained U.S. leadership in the air. This leadership goal for our nation was first and foremost at the root of Lindbergh's dedicated motivation, and of his personal sacrifices for its attainment.

In recounting Lindbergh's contributions to air transportation, one could go through volumes of aviation history. Or, one could find the flavor and thrust of these achievements expressed in a single handwritten report he sent from Reykjavik, Iceland, to his friend and associate, Juan T. Trippe of Pan American in New York on 18 August 1933.

The thoughts he expressed in that letter are prophetic, particularly when we recall that it was written nearly forty-five years ago, during a pioneering survey flight of the northern transatlantic air route used frequently by today's jet airliners.

In establishing a transatlantic air route, it is fully as important to decide which route will be most advantageous in the future as it is to decide which is the best to operate over today. It must be remembered that the route which is best for our present equipment and experience will not necessarily be as good as some other route when we have more efficient aircraft and have learned more about transoceanic flying.

When Lindbergh wrote this report in 1933, many thought that only amphibians and seaplanes could be used in long overwater routes, but he looked to the future:

I believe that whether eventual operation of any important air line be with land planes or flying boats will be decided largely by their speed and payload. If the land plane has a decided advantage, in this respect, I believe it will replace other types and that ways can be found of carrying on the operation of land planes with safety, even over water.

Was he predicting in 1933 the advent of today's jet airliner? Perhaps, for he wrote in that same report: "I believe that in the future aircraft will detour bad weather areas by flying above them rather than around them."

Today, in 1977, air transportation, although it enables people and commerce to move speedily and safely over the barriers of time and distance, seems lately to be preoccupied with some rather down-to-earth concerns — ranging from pressing problems of capital formation and the industry's regulatory future to noise abatement and the conservative use of dwindling fuel supplies. Surveying Lindbergh's contributions to air transportation gives us a chance temporarily to set these concerns aside and to look again and reflect on the soaring successes of air transportation and on its contribution to the quality of life.

Lindbergh made so many flights to promote and nurture the development of air transportation because he had so many goals he thought a budding industry should and could achieve:

The demonstrated ability to provide safe, regular and dependable, on-time service; a nationwide system of good airports; growth of air mail, in the strong conviction that volume passenger traffic would inevitably follow; careful exploration and mapping of new air routes throughout the nation and worldwide, as a vital step in securing U.S. leadership in air transportation; development of an airways system for good navigation and communication between the air and the ground; fuel-efficient and otherwise more productive aircraft; thorough training for airline flight crews; and finally, a sense of balance in the development of air transportation to ensure its contribution to the quality of life.

I will not attempt a chronological listing of all of Lindbergh's contributions to air transportation. But we should take the opportunity to examine what he thought and said should be done to assure U.S. world leadership in air transportation—always his primary goal. At the beginning of the second fifty years of scheduled airline service, pursuit of this goal remains a guideline for the future growth of air transportation.

One of Lindbergh's biographers has written that, to his wife Anne, Lindbergh was "a poet who wrote his verses in the sky and did it with his own kind of music." Certainly, there was much of the poet's music in the solo transatlantic flight he began fifty years ago. It excited the world and lifted the prospects of air transportation more than any other flight, before or since.

Only two months later, in the summer of 1927, Lindbergh began a nation-wide air tour in the *Spirit of St. Louis* to promote air transportation. The tour, under the auspices of The Daniel Guggenheim Fund for the Promotion of Aeronautics, whatever the immediacy of its excitement and tumult, had a number of well thought out long-range objectives.

Arriving at each city on time was a key objective. Lindbergh wanted to show to acclaiming crowds that scheduled air transportation could be as reliable as the crack trains in that golden age of passenger rail travel.

The same plane and engine that had successfully carried him across the Atlantic were used on the long U. S. tour to demonstrate aircraft reliability, and Lindbergh provided an early preview of flight planning by carefully selecting altitudes to overcome adverse weather conditions.

Leonard Mosley, one of Lindbergh's biographers, said Lindbergh "believed that by showing himself and the *Spirit of St. Louis* to the people and always arriving on time, no matter what the weather, he would prove to them that the air age had arrived and that they should become part of it." He did and they followed.

From the time Lindbergh took off from New York on 20 July 1927, until he returned to Mitchel Field, Long Island, on 23 October of that year, he covered 22,350 miles. He visited eighty-two cities, covering all of the then forty-eight states. He missed only one scheduled appearance—at Portland, Maine, due to extremely heavy fog.

Better than any summary are some of Lindbergh's own words on behalf of air transportation during his epoch-making 1927 national air tour. For an example of his expansive view on air transportation, consider his concluding paragraph from a message he would sometimes drop in a canvas bag flying over communities he could not visit personally.

> We feel that we will be amply repaid for our efforts if each and every citizen in the United States cherishes an interest in flying and gives his earnest support to the Air Mail Service and the establishment of airports and similar facilities. The concerted efforts of the citizens of the United States in this direction will result in America's taking its rightful place, within a very short time, as the world leader of commercial flying.

Note again his commitment to world leadership.

His comments in the scores of communities where he did stop show a remarkably prophetic vision of air transportation. Consider the following from a news conference in Hartford, as reported in the *New York Times* of 21 July 1927. Drawing a parallel between communities that would build airports on the one hand, and communities on main rail lines and on the highways being built in that day, on the other hand, he said, "The places that have airports will be far ahead of those without them."

Passenger service will follow the mail service. . . . The time when there will be an air service available for all who want to use it depends upon what use you make of the present air facilities. We now have a mail service that is struggling for existence and with 50 per cent more cooperation and assistance from the public it would be a great success.

Looking beyond the boundaries of the United States and always the realist, Lindbergh said that transatlantic air service would not come in the near future, but in ten or fifteen years.

His prediction about transatlantic air service was on target. On 20 May 1939, exactly twelve years from the day on which Lindbergh took off on his historic flight to Paris, Pan Am's new flying boat, the *Yankee Clipper,* took off from New York to Lisbon. In inaugurating this regularly scheduled transatlantic air service, the *Yankee Clipper* used a route that had been mapped by Lindbergh and his wife, Anne, who was so often at his side in those pioneer days of commercial aviation.

The airports that Lindbergh urged communities to build in 1927 were built. They have evolved from simple landing strips to become complex transportation centers. They have made possible the growth of many cities and have become major contributors to local economies.

Altitude selection and other flight-planning skills demonstrated by Lindbergh have grown into a computer-backed science. He was keenly involved in developments that led to computerized flight planning used, not only for safety and passenger comfort, but also in conserving millions of gallons of fuel annually.

Fifty years after his demonstration flights of 1927, the legacy of on-time performance remains. On the 13,000 daily flights operated today by the U.S. airlines, on-time arrivals and departures continue as a hallmark of a transportation system widely recognized as the best in the world.

The growth in the air transportation of mail foreseen by Lindbergh has been achieved. In 1977, the airlines will transport eight out of every ten pieces of intercity first-class mail and millions of air parcel post packages.

As Lindbergh had foreseen, passengers did follow the mail, and in ever-increasing numbers so that air transportation has been the predominant form of intercity passenger travel for about two decades. The airlines today account for more than eighty percent of public passenger travel between cities in this country and more than ninety percent between the United States and points overseas. In 1976, the U.S. airlines carried a record 223 million passengers; this total will be exceeded by perhaps another six percent or more in 1977, based on current forecasts.

In available service and the network of points served, in lower costs for the users and in production of airline aircraft and engines, the United States is the world leader — the fulfillment of Lindbergh's driving commitment. His was a prophecy that has come true.

Making the prophecy come true — turning vision to reality — required difficult spadework back in the late twenties and early thirties. Part of the spadework involved the mapping of new air routes, a task Lindbergh performed for Transcontinental Air Transport (later to become TWA) and for Pan Am.

One of Lindbergh's chief responsibilities as chairman of Transcontinental's technical committee was to supervise the organization and mapping of a coast-to-coast route system. The indefatigable Lindberghs also mapped routes for Pam Am from the United States to the Caribbean and South America, and to Asia, Europe, and Africa.

The flight they made in laying out the great circle route north to the Orient was certainly one of the most dramatic. It began 27 July 1931. They flew up the coast of Maine, across Canada and Alaska, across the Bering Strait, down the coast to Siberia, to the Chishima Island chain of Japan, on to Tokyo and from Japan across the Yellow Sea to China. They flew up the flooding Yangtze and landed on 19 September 1931, on Lotus Lake outside Nanking.

Although this route was 1,200 miles shorter than the mid-Pacific route, some wondered why the Lindberghs had undertaken such a grueling air expedition. Anne Morrow Lindbergh gave at least part of the answer when she wrote:

> Our route was new; the air untraveled; the stories mythical; the maps pale, pink and indefinite, except for a few names far to the east of our course, to show that someone before pointed his ship, also, North to the Orient.

An incredible amount of planning went into Lindbergh's early survey flights, and he insisted on even more detailed planning before actual bases were selected and scheduled service commenced. Let's return for a moment to the reports he sent back to Juan Trippe in 1933 while surveying the northern transatlantic route.

To gain more knowledge, he urged experimental flying "between points on definitely laid out routes rather than taking off and returning to the same base."

He urged multiengine aircraft, "in the interest of safety," and stressed that before sending planes over the northern route, "the personnel should be thoroughly experienced in northern flying and a competent ground organization established." He went into this subject so thoroughly as to urge in a report from Stockholm on 15 September 1933, that "it is of utmost importance to use only personnel who like the north country and who have confidence in its future."

He urged extensive work in developing landing fields and an adequate network of radio stations. Even in suggesting possible sites for bases on the northern transatlantic route, Lindbergh cautioned: "I want to point out to you again, however, that a careful meteorological study must precede any final decision."

Some of the incidents encountered on these early route development flights offered signposts for latter-day air transportation. There was the time late in 1931, for example, when Lindbergh had piloted Pan Am's new amphibian flying boat, the *American Clipper,* to Barranquilla, Colombia, only to find the runway so crowded with excited and curious crowds that he couldn't land. What to do? The skilled and resourceful airman calmly landed on a lake some distance away and then, with the help of a native canoe and horse, he delivered a sack of mail to the Colombian city. A combination of air mail and pony express, Lindbergh's delivery offered an interesting early example of the intermodal transportation airlines would later use to give cargo both the speed of air transportation and the convenience of door-to-door delivery.

Some of the early work in commercial aviation development was less glamorous than mapping new air routes but equally important. Lindbergh helped select future airline pilots and helped establish standards for their rigorous training. Under his direction, better lighting and other equipment was installed at airports, and the ground-to-air radio communication was inaugurated that later became part of the intricate air traffic control system.

Improving the margin of safety was paramount then, as it is today. When

Lindbergh recommended that TWA purchase the DC-1, he imposed the extra requirement that the plane be able to take off with a full load using only one engine, that it be able to do this at any point in the TWA system, and that it be able to maintain level flight on one engine over the highest mountains on the airline's routes.

There were other goals he sought for air transportation then that also remain timely today, as timely as the continuing quest for more fuel-efficient engines. Pan Am's founder, Juan Trippe, with whom Lindbergh worked closely for more than forty years, recalled in a recent conversation that Lindbergh insisted that fuel consumption and other characteristics of new engines be economically justified:

> *What pleased Slim most was to keep the United States ahead of the world in commercial aviation technology. He stressed that the emphasis in research, development and manufacture must focus strongly on economic justification. That fundamental consideration was always in his mind, whether a new design involved an engine or seating configuration.*

Charles Lindbergh's flight across the Atlantic on 20 May 1927, and each flight he made thereafter, had a purpose: to establish and secure for our country a safe, reliable, and comprehensive air transportation system, second to none, and dedicated to a better way of life for all of us. With vision and realism, Lindbergh has given us a rich legacy in the skies.

The following materials were consulted
in the preparation of this paper.

1. Harry Bruno, *Wings over America: The Story of American Aviation* (Garden City, N.Y.: Halcyon House, 1944).

2. R. E. G. Davies, *Airlines of the United States since 1914* (London: Putnam, 1972).

3. R. E. G. Davies, *A History of the World's Airlines* (London: Oxford University Press, 1964).

4. Matthew Josephson, *Empire of the Air: Juan Trippe and the Struggle for World Airways* (New York: Harcourt Brace, 1944).

5. Lt. Donald Keyhoe, U.S.M.C. (Ret.), "Seeing America with Lindbergh," *National Geographic Magazine* (January 1928).

6. Anne M. Lindbergh, *Hour of Gold, Hour of Lead: Diaries and Letters of Anne Morrow Lindbergh, 1929–1932* (New York: Harcourt Brace Jovanovich, 1973).

7. Anne M. Lindbergh, *North to the Orient* (New York: Harcourt Brace, 1935).

8. Charles A. Lindbergh, *The Spirit of St. Louis* (New York: Charles Scribner's Sons, 1953).

9. Leonard Mosley, *Lindbergh: A Biography* (New York: Doubleday, 1976).

10. *New York Times,* 21 July 1927.

11. Henry Ladd Smith, *Airways* (New York: Russell & Russell, 1965).

12. Juan T. Trippe, "Ocean Air Transport," *Journal of the Royal Aeronautical Society 45* (September 1941).

13. Trans World Airlines, Flight Operations Department, *Legacy of Leadership* (Marceline, Mo.: Walsworth, 1970).

14. Correspondence between Charles A. Lindbergh and Juan T. Trippe, Pan American World Airways, Inc., N.Y.

PAUL R. IGNATIUS joined the Air Transport Association in February 1972 as executive vice president, and in December 1972 was elected president by the ATA board of directors. In December 1973, he was also elected chief executive officer.

Before joining ATA, Ignatius was president of *The Washington Post* from 1969 to 1971. He was appointed Secretary of the Navy in September 1967, and served in that position until January 1969. Before becoming Secretary of the Navy, he had served as Assistant Secretary of the Army for Installations and Logistics in 1961, Undersecretary of the Army from February to December 1964, and Assistant Secretary of Defense for Installations and Logistics from 1964 to 1967. Before his federal service, he was vice president and a director of Harbridge House, a management consulting firm in Massachusetts.

Paul Ignatius has a bachelor's degree from the University of Southern California and a master's degree in business administration from Harvard University.

A native of Los Angeles, he is married and lives in Washington, D.C.

Charles Lindbergh was the most photographed public figure of his era. As the lean young man with the infectious grin posing beside a silver monoplane; the path-finding pilot of the thirties; the impassioned spokesman for peace; or the postwar voice of environmental sanity, his face remained familiar to the readers of American newspapers and magazines for almost half a century.

Born in Detroit, Lindbergh, shown here with his mother in about 1908, grew up in Little Falls, Minnesota, near the headwaters of the Mississippi.

He made his first flight on 9 April 1922, seated beside his friend Bud Gurney in the front cockpit of a Lincoln Standard Turnabout.

Anxious to pilot high-performance aircraft, Lindbergh abandoned his short barnstorming career to enlist as an aviation cadet in April 1924. These photos show him during his flight training at Brooks and Kelly Fields, near San Antonio, Texas.

Top man in his class, he received a commission as a second lieutenant in the Army Air Service Reserve in March 1925.

Now a thoroughly trained aviator, Lindbergh joined Robertson Air Lines of Saint Louis as chief pilot. He first conceived the possibility of flying from New York to Paris during a flight on the Saint Louis–Chicago mail run in one of the DH-4 mail planes flown by Robertson.

One of the pilots Lindbergh hired to assist him was Phil Love, an old friend from Army flying school.

OVERLEAF
In addition to flying the mail, Lindbergh instructed student pilots like W. G. Smith, shown here.

Following a series of test flights in California, Lindbergh broke crosscountry speed records as he flew from San Diego to New York. He is shown here at take-off from Lambert Field, Saint Louis on 12 May 1927.

During test flights from Curtiss Field, New York, on 14 May, Lindbergh established optimum fuel mixture settings with the aid of Curtiss-Wright engineers.

Early on the morning of 20 May the Spirit was towed from Curtiss to Roosevelt Field, where the gasoline tanks were topped off in preparation for take-off.

The immortal Spirit of St. Louis *was constructed by Ryan Airlines, of San Diego, California, in only 60 days. Lindbergh and his Saint Louis backers paid $10,580 for the craft.*

Although Washington, D.C., was the first port-of-call during Lindbergh's triumphant return tour of the United States, New York Mayor James J. Walker insisted that the young aviator enter his city with a harbor reception. An estimated 300,000 spectators viewed this scene from the Battery. (Photo from Mrs. M. K. Parkhurst)

Not to be outdone, citizens of Saint Louis welcomed their adopted son home on 17 June 1927.

Charles A. Lindbergh
and Aviation Technology

RICHARD P. HALLION

Without question, Charles Lindbergh is a complex historical figure. His career and personality were both multifaceted, and he presented an often perplexing public image that inevitably forced observers to ask, "Who *is* the real Charles Lindbergh?" Was it the boyish hero, "Lucky Lindy, the Lone Eagle," the "eventful" man who provided Jazz-Age America with a desperately needed symbol? Or was it Lindbergh the prewar political figure and social commentator? What of Lindbergh the unsettled citizen searching for solitude and privacy? Or Lindbergh the airman? Perhaps Lindbergh the colleague of Alexis Carrel and acquaintance of Teilhard de Chardin? Could Lindbergh the environmentalist and defender of primitive societies be the one?

The answer, of course, is that Lindbergh encompassed all of these. His was the idealized existence of Renaissance Man; his temperament and restlessness did not permit him to develop a limited world view. Like the Renaissance figure, he appreciated politics, philosophy, literature, nature, religion, military affairs, science, and technology. Of all these Lindberghs, the one that we most often tend to forget is Charles Augustus Lindbergh, flight technologist.

It is hard to think of a pilot who began as a barnstormer and parachutist as a contributor to flight technology and the technical development of modern aviation. With Lindbergh, however, such is the case. His broad perspective did not permit him the luxury of becoming an exponent of unchecked scientific and technological growth. Reflecting on a test flight he performed during World War II, Lindbergh wrote in 1948, "In worshipping science man gains power but loses the quality of life." [1] In his remarks on accepting the Daniel Guggenheim Medal for 1953, Lindbergh commented on the growing cold war and cautioned, "Short-term survival may depend on the knowledge of nuclear physicists and

---

1. Charles A. Lindbergh, *Of Flight and Life* (New York: Charles Scribner's Sons, 1948), p. 10.

the performance of supersonic aircraft, but long-term survival depends alone on the character of man."[2]

Lindbergh's grasp of aeronautical technology first appeared during the design of the Ryan NYP monoplane that he flew to Paris. His first concern was flight efficiency. He rejected use of a multiengine aircraft for reasons of safety, complexity, and aerodynamics, preferring a single-seat, single-engine, high-performance monoplane. The fuel tank location eliminated all forward vision. In a bid to reduce airframe drag, Lindbergh accepted this and selected a retractable periscope that he could extend when he needed a forward view. He selected a Wright J5C Whirlwind radial piston engine, as it promised high power, good fuel consumption characteristics, and great reliability. He selected the cockpit instrumentation with care, and the instrument panel of the *Spirit of St. Louis* had the best long-range instrumentation display of its time.[3] Unlike many airmen who contested for the Raymond Orteig Prize, Lindbergh was not simply a pilot ordering a special aircraft from some manufacturer. He participated fully as a member of the design team, and the resulting aircraft reflected as much his desires and thoughts as it did those of Ryan project engineer Donald Hall. The epochal flight across the Atlantic was the result of Lindbergh's meticulous planning. It required daring, courage, skill, and, above all, thorough preparation. The aircraft that emerged from the Lindbergh-Hall partnership was clearly the most advanced long-range airplane of its time. It affirmed the ascendency of the monoplane configuration and the radial engine and the growing strength of American aeronautical technology.

Lindbergh's actions on his return to America were more important technologically to the advance of aviation than the flight itself. At the behest of Harry F. Guggenheim, president of The Daniel Guggenheim Fund for the Promotion of Aeronautics, a philanthropic fund that furthered aviation in the

2. Acceptance Address by Charles A. Lindbergh of the Daniel Guggenheim Medal, at the Honors Night Dinner of the Institute of the Aeronautical Sciences, New York, 25 January 1954.

3. Charles A. Lindbergh, *The Spirit of St. Louis* (New York: Charles Scribner's Sons, 1953), pp. 17–18, 20, 25–26, 28–29, 59–61, 69, 81, 87; H. Guyford Stever and James J. Haggerty, *Flight* (New York: Time-Life Books, 1965), p. 126; R. A. Chorley, "Seventy Years of Flight Instruments and Displays," 3d H. P. Folland Memorial Lecture, Presented to the Royal Aeronautical Society, Gloucester and Cheltenham Branch, England, 19 February 1976; Donald A. Hall, *Technical Note No. 257: Technical Preparation of the Airplane,* Spirit of St. Louis (Washington, D.C.: National Advisory Committee for Aeronautics, July 1927).

1920s to a greater degree than any other single factor, he made a tour of the country to promote the use of air mail and foster public acceptance of commercial aviation. Lindbergh flew to all of the then forty-eight states, covering a distance of 22,350 miles. More than 30 million people saw the famed aviator and listened while he promoted air mail, local airport construction, and town marking as an aid to navigation. Lindbergh's impact on the air mail service is vividly illustrated by the following statistics: In May 1927, mail planes carried 99,107 lbs. of mail. In June this jumped to 118,746 lbs., rising to 146,000 lbs. in September of 1927. William MacCracken, Assistant Secretary of the Department of Commerce, credited Lindbergh with the increased use of air mail, inspiring municipalities to acquire or improve existing airports and demonstrating the reliability of then-current aircraft.[4] Ahead lay Lindbergh's goodwill tour to Mexico, Central and South America, and finally enshrinement of the plane at the Smithsonian Institution in Washington, D.C.

The nationwide tour marked the beginning of Lindbergh's involvement with the Guggenheim Fund. He joined the fund as a trustee and participated as an advisor on most subsequent fund programs. When Harry Guggenheim planned a model airline experiment on the West Coast, he consulted with Lindbergh before selecting the Fokker F-10 trimotor subsequently built for Western Air Express's use on the trial service. Lindbergh also advised Guggenheim on such research topics as blind flight and short-take-off-and-landing aircraft development. Though the Guggenheim Fund disbanded in 1930, Lindbergh continued to bring Harry Guggenheim up to date on aeronautical development.

It was in this role as an informal Guggenheim consultant that Charles Lindbergh made one of his most important contributions to aerospace science: He brought Robert H. Goddard to the attention of Daniel and Harry Guggenheim. Goddard, a visionary who firmly believed in the future of rocket propulsion, had launched the world's first liquid-fuel rocket in March 1926. Lindbergh, too, was interested in rocketry. The famed aviator had concluded during a crosscountry survey flight in 1928 that reaction-powered aircraft would eventually replace propeller-driven planes. As a start, he was interested in whether a rocket engine could be used to provide emergency power equivalent

4. Department of Commerce, "Lindbergh Tour Great Boost to Commercial Aeronautics," 13 July 1927, Charles A. Lindbergh Folder, Box 52, Hoover Papers, Herbert Hoover Presidential Library, West Branch, Ia.; Richard P. Hallion, *Legacy of Flight: The Guggenheim Contribution to American Aviation* (Seattle: University of Washington Press, 1977), pp. 152, 154–58, 159.

to the power of a Wasp piston engine for one minute's operation, should an airplane lose conventional engine power in flight, especially after take-off. In mid-1929, he visited Du Pont company engineers, who flicked their slide rules and concluded that such a rocket engine would require 400 lbs. of black powder igniting in a firebrick-lined combustion chamber. In November 1929, Lindbergh learned of Goddard's work from a press account. He immediately contacted the scientist and became convinced that Goddard was on the right road to practical rocket propulsion.

Lindbergh succeeded in getting the Carnegie Institute to issue Goddard a small grant. The aviator realized, however, that Goddard needed much more money than the limited funding available, and in the spring of 1930, he approached Daniel Guggenheim. The old entrepreneur listened then asked Lindbergh if Goddard's work would advance aeronautical science. Lindbergh replied that one could never be certain, but that Goddard knew more about rocketry than anyone else in the United States. Without further hesitation, the elder Guggenheim pledged $100,000 from his own funds for Goddard's research in a move that Lindbergh later termed "highly visionary and very courageous."[5] Daniel Guggenheim died later that year, and, in 1932, Goddard's initial Guggenheim funding came to an end. Once again, Lindbergh stepped into the breach; he convinced Harry Guggenheim to continue support of the rocket pioneer via the Daniel and Florence Guggenheim Foundation. From then until Goddard joined the Navy's rocket research effort during World War II, Lindbergh was a frequent visitor at Goddard's Roswell, New Mexico, test site. Goddard's breadth of vision was such that future rocket and missile manufacturers and designers found that they could not design, construct, or operate a rocket-propelled vehicle without infringing on one or more of Goddard's patents. Charles Lindbergh never had the opportunity to see a live launching of a Goddard rocket. It is fitting that in July 1969 he did have the privilege of watching Apollo 11 thunder aloft from the Cape on its way to the first lunar landing, though one naturally wishes that Goddard could have been there beside him.

5. Conversation with Charles A. Lindbergh, 22 July 1974. *See also* Milton Lehman, *This High Man: The Life of Robert H. Goddard* (New York: Farrar, Straus, 1963), pp. 173–74; Milton Lomask, *Seed Money: The Guggenheim Story* (New York: Farrar, Straus & Giroux, 1964), pp. 141–42; Charles A. Lindbergh, introduction, in Michael Collins, *Carrying the Fire* (New York: Farrar, Straus & Giroux, 1974), pp. ix–xiii; Hallion, *Legacy of Flight,* pp. 174–76.

Before his wartime service, Lindbergh's next major technical contribution came as an advisor to the airlines on air transportation matters. He acted chiefly on behalf of Transcontinental Air Transport (a forerunner to TWA) and of Pan American Airways. This involved furnishing technical inputs on airline decision making and also flying the routes, both those planned and those in use. His survey flights, made in partnership with his wife, Anne Morrow Lindbergh, who acted as radio operator and navigator, attracted the greatest attention from the press. Lindbergh's supervision of Transcontinental Air Transport's national air-route network development was so established that TAT became known as the "Lindbergh Line." He flew all through the United States, the Caribbean, and Central and South America. Two flights in particular deserve special mention. In July 1931, the Lindberghs began a flight to the Orient via the great circle route over the Arctic down to Japan and China, a polar route basically similar to the one followed by many airliners today. In 1933, the Lindberghs again flew a pioneering survey flight, this one to Greenland, Europe, Russia, Africa, and South America, for Pan American, to acquire information useful in establishing commercial air routes across the North and South Atlantic. The flight provided knowledge on requirements for landing fields, radio airway aids, and meteorological reporting services. The Lindbergh airplane, a modified Lockheed Sirius floatplane named *Tingmissartoq* (Eskimo for "one who flies like a big bird") is now on exhibit at the National Air and Space Museum, together with the *Spirit of St. Louis*.[6]

While acting as technical advisor to Pan American, Lindbergh supervised Pan Am's introduction of blind-flying instrumentation flight techniques over that airline's routes. He also participated in technical decisions pertaining to acquiring new aircraft and was, initially, an enthusiastic advocate of the long-range flying boat. Lindbergh's interest in flying boats stemmed from his strong friendship with aviation pioneer Igor Sikorsky. Often the two men would spend hours planning what new flying boats should look like, and, as consultant to Pan Am's Juan Trippe, Lindbergh was tremendously influential in the design and development of the first really large Sikorsky flying boat, the four-engine S-40, the first of which, the *American Clipper*, Lindbergh flew to South America in late 1931. Yet Lindbergh was not as inflexible as many other flying boat

6. A good account of this first survey flight is to be found in Anne Morrow Lindbergh's memoir, *North to the Orient* (New York: Harcourt, Brace, 1935).

supporters; he recognized the limitations under which flying boats operated, and, when a rim of concrete airfields sprang up on tidal shores around the world, he became an equally strong advocate of the long-range landplane, which eventually came to dominate international air commerce.[7]

His connection to Transcontinental and Western Air, the successor to TAT and immediate forerunner to Trans World Airlines, had an interesting effect on one aircraft of particular significance in aviation history, the Douglas DC-1. In 1932, TWA had approached Douglas about designing a new passenger airplane that could replace the outmoded trimotor aircraft then in service and could rival the projected Boeing 247 then under development. As one of the company's technical advisors, Lindbergh convinced the airline to require Douglas to design the twin-engine plane to execute single-engine take-offs with a full load from any of the airports along TWA's routes. Though this taxed the Douglas company's engineering skills, Lindbergh's goal was achieved. Encouraged by the performance of the DC-1, Douglas placed the larger-capacity DC-2 in quantity production and followed with the legendary DC-3, the most successful airliner of all time. Lindbergh's insistence on single-engine operational capability for the DC-1 paved the way for the DC-3 to fly with maximum safety, efficiency, and economy.[8]

In 1931, Charles Lindbergh became a member of the National Advisory Committee for Aeronautics (NACA), the national aeronautical research establishment. He conferred frequently with aviation experts on various problems, and Vannevar Bush, chairman of NACA, was apparently so impressed with Lindbergh's technical competence that in 1939 he asked the flyer if he would be interested in the chairmanship. (Lindbergh declined, stating that his greatest interests lay in other fields and that he did not wish to devote his entire attention to aviation.)[9] While with NACA, Lindbergh pressed vigorously for a comprehensive national aeronautical research and development policy aimed at

7. Frank J. Delear, *Igor Sikorsky: His Three Careers in Aviation* (New York: Dodd, Mead & Co., 1976), pp. 137, 142–53, 166–67; Juan T. Trippe, "Ocean Air Transport," 29th Wilbur Wright Memorial Lecture, Presented to the Royal Aeronautical Society, London, England, 17 June 1941.

8. Douglas J. Ingells, *The Plane that Changed the World: A Biography of the DC-3* (Fallbrook, Calif.: Aero Publishers, 1966), pp. 18–19, 26–36.

9. Charles A. Lindbergh, *The Wartime Journals of Charles A. Lindbergh* (New York: Harcourt Brace Jovanovich, 1970), p. 208.

ensuring that American aircraft remained competitive with their foreign counterparts. He was instrumental in the establishment of the Ames Aeronautical Laboratory. As chairman of a NACA committee on the laboratory proposal, Lindbergh argued cogently for its creation in the face of aircraft industry apathy and, in some cases, active opposition. Now the NASA Ames Research Center, this facility has had major impact on American aerospace development, especially in the field of reentry technology.[10]

Though his isolationist policies gained him great notoriety, once Japan attacked Pearl Harbor, Lindbergh would lobby with equal fervor to get into the war effort. At first he served as a technical troubleshooter with the Ford Motor Company. As early as April 1942 he was involved in readying the B-24 bomber for combat. He performed high-altitude engine ignition trials in an experimental P-47 and undertook detailed studies of human physiological behavior during simulated high-altitude flight in conjunction with the Mayo Foundation.[11] Next he joined United Aircraft Corporation as a consultant, devoting his attention to making the F4U Corsair fighter a combatworthy aircraft.

One of the earliest proponents of turbojet propulsion, Lindbergh actively supported turbojet aircraft design studies by Vought company engineers.[12] Then, in April 1944, he went overseas. While in the South Pacific as a civilian advisor to the Navy and Army Air Forces, Lindbergh completed fifty combat missions and shot down a Japanese fighter. He refined long-range cruise control techniques, allowing American P-38 fighters to increase their combat radius from 570 to 750 miles by careful fuel and engine-power management. He also developed techniques enabling Marine Corsairs to carry up to 4,000 lbs. of bombs, testing this arrangement (the largest bombload carried by a single-engine fighter up to that time) in actual strike missions against Japanese targets.[13] After the collapse of Nazi Germany, United Aircraft Corporation asked Lindbergh to tour Germany as a member of the Naval Technical Mission in

10. Ibid., pp. 214–15, 217, 229; Edwin P. Hartman, *Adventures in Research: A History of the Ames Research Center, 1940–1965* (Washington, D.C.: National Aeronautics and Space Administration, 1970), pp. 16–22.

11. Lindbergh, *Wartime Journals,* pp. 627–731.

12. Ibid., pp. 756, 762–63, 774.

13. Ibid., pp. 787–929, (esp. 872–73, 880, 911–12, 918, 920–22).

Europe. During his time in Germany, Lindbergh visited German aeronautical research establishments and met with and interviewed a number of aeronautical authorities, including Helmut Schelp, Willy Messerschmitt, Waldemar Voigt Felix Kracht, and Adolf Busemann. He then collaborated with other investigators on a summary report on German wartime aeronautical research and development. This report, submitted to the government, advocated broad postwar American aerospace research programs.[14]

After World War II, Air Force Chief General Carl Spaatz asked Lindbergh to serve as a special consultant on research and development for the Air Force. It was the kind of position that Lindbergh relished, and he accepted with pleasure. He helped map out efficient methods of operation for the Berlin Airlift effort, participated with John von Neumann of the Air Force Scientific Advisory Board on nuclear weapon and ballistic missile studies, and served as a member of H. Guyford Stever's Scientific Advisory Board panel on ballistic missile defense. He contributed to two major SAB reports in 1955 and 1956. He also participated in base selection and reorganization planning for the Strategic Air Command and made familiarization flights in SAC's B-52 bombers. He worked with the Army and the University of Chicago on the Project CHORE ordnance study, which influenced development of new air-to-air weapon systems. For his valuable work with the Department of Defense, President Eisenhower restored Lindbergh's commission, which the flyer had resigned before World War II. Lindbergh became an Air Force Reserve brigadier general in April 1954. He continued his interest in aviation medicine, now combining it with enthusiasm over manned space flight, and he worked closely with aerospace medical pioneer Hubertus Strughold.[15]

14. Ibid., pp. 933–1000; Walter S. Ross, *The Last Hero: Charles A. Lindbergh* (New York: Harper & Row, 1968), pp. 328–29, 332; Leonard Mosley, *Lindbergh: A Biography* (Garden City, N.Y.: Doubleday & Co., 1976), pp. 328–35, 342–43; C. F. Cotton, *Technical Report No. 373–45: German War Research vs. Air Superiority* (U.S. Naval Technical Mission in Europe, September 1945).

15. Lindbergh, *Wartime Journals*, p. xiv; Mosley, *Lindbergh*, pp. 343–48, 352–54; John Grierson, "Charles A. Lindbergh: A Pioneer Remembered," Lindbergh Memorial Lecture, Presented to the Royal Aeronautical Society, the Royal Aero Club, and the Guild of Air Pilots and Air Navigators, London, England, 21 May 1975; Thomas A. Sturm, *The USAF Scientific Advisory Board: Its First Twenty Years, 1944–1964* (Washington, D.C.: U.S.A.F. Historical Liaison Office, 1967), p. 167.

Along with his military affiliations, Lindbergh continued to act as consultant with Pan American, advising in that airline's acquisition of America's first jet transport, the revolutionary Boeing 707. Yet Lindbergh never allowed himself to become carried away by an emotional attachment to rampant technological expansion. He participated in Pan Am's initial discussions on development of a supersonic transport, but when it appeared that a first-generation SST would cost a great deal to develop and operate and have a potentially deleterious effect on the environment that Lindbergh so highly valued, he became an outspoken opponent. Pan Am subsequently rejected acquisition of American or foreign SST aircraft. Ill health forced Lindbergh's resignation from Pan Am's board of directors in 1974, and he died in August of that year at the age of 72.[16]

How can one categorize Lindbergh as a technologist? Once again the Renaissance metaphor comes to mind. Lindbergh's approach to technology ranged from the hands-on tinkering of a mechanic to the incisive methodological research of a scientist. He used the terms "science" and "technology" virtually interchangeably, consistent with his Baconian view that science exists for the good of humanity and his implicit acceptance of Francis Bacon's dictum that the goal of science is the manifestation of works. He ventured in other fields besides aeronautics, and his collaboration with Alexis Carrel resulting in the perfusion pump had truly great significance for medical technology.[17] He was a humanist, a naturalist, and an anthropologist. His environmental concerns stemmed from a deep-rooted respect for nature that bordered on pantheism. He recognized the narrow margin on which society trod in the unstable nuclear era, and his work after World War II confirmed his fear that humanity now had the ability to destroy in minutes what previous generations had taken centuries to create. And so Lindbergh the technologist changed to Lindbergh the philosopher, protector of the Tasaday, preaching a turn from materialistic, mechanistic society toward a society based on "simplicity, humility, contemplation, prayer. It requires a dedication beyond science, beyond self, but the rewards are great and it is our

16. Lindbergh to Rep. Emilio Q. Daddario, 1 July 1970, and Lindbergh to Rep. Sidney R. Yates, 3 February 1971, Charles A. Lindbergh Papers, Sterling Memorial Library, Yale University, New Haven, Conn.

17. "Pioneer Flyer Advanced Medicine by Designing Organ Perfusion Pump," *Journal of the American Medical Association* 237 (23 May 1977): 2270.

48

only hope." [18] Coming from others, such sentiments could easily sound artificial and forced. Coming from Charles Lindbergh, they carried the tone of conviction and sincere belief, hallmarks of a great man.

RICHARD P. HALLION is associate curator of science and technology at the National Air and Space Museum. He received his Ph.D. in history from the University of Maryland in 1975. He is the author of two books, *Supersonic Flight: Breaking the Sound Barrier and Beyond* (1972) and *Legacy of Flight: The Guggenheim Contribution to American Aviation* (1977), and of numerous articles and monographs. He won the 1975 History Manuscript Award of the American Institute of Aeronautics and Astronautics. Hallion was privileged to converse at length with Charles Lindbergh on Guggenheim aviation activities scant months before the pioneer aviator died and has had access to the Lindbergh Papers at Yale.

18. Lindbergh, *Of Flight and Life,* p. 55.

Charles A. Lindbergh
and the Battle against Intervention

WAYNE S. COLE

Everyone loves a winner. But what happens when a winner becomes a loser? More to the point, what happens when a winner becomes a loser on behalf of a discredited cause that is seen as naive or even treasonous? And what happens when those charges come from "the best and the brightest," from the most literate and vocal opinion-shapers? Such was the experience of Charles A. Lindbergh in opposing American entry into World War II. Lindbergh demonstrated his courage, his character, his stubborn independence, his patriotism, and his heroism fully as much in his losing battle against American entry into World War II as he did in his winning battle to conquer the skies over the Atlantic a half century ago.[1]

The background and course of Colonel Lindbergh's battle against intervention may be sketched briefly. In December 1935, after the tragic kidnapping and murder of their son, Charles and Anne Lindbergh quietly slipped out of the country with their second son. They sought temporary refuge in England and later in France from the harassment they had suffered in the United States at the hands of newsmen, curiosity-seekers, and crackpots. During more than three years abroad, Colonel Lindbergh availed himself of unique opportunities to study military aviation developments in Europe. The United States military attaché in Berlin arranged the invitations that brought Lindbergh to Germany. During three major visits, he inspected all the types of combat planes that Germany was to use in the first two years of World War II. He piloted some of those planes before the war, including the Me-109 fighter. His findings on German air power were reported to the highest leadership levels in the United States, Great Britain, and France. In cooperation with officials, he also inspected

---

1. Portions of this account were included in my earlier address, Wayne S. Cole, "A Tale of Two Isolationists — Told Three Wars Later," *The Society for Historians of American Foreign Relations Newsletter* 5 (March 1974): 2–16; for a more detailed treatment, *see* Wayne S. Cole, *Charles A. Lindbergh and the Battle against American Intervention in World War II* (New York and London: Harcourt Brace Jovanovich, 1974).

aviation developments in England, France, the Soviet Union, and Czecho-slovakia.[2]

As a result, Colonel Lindbergh became convinced that Germany was the natural air power in Europe, and that German air power surpassed that of all other European states. He was troubled by the contrast between the decadence he thought he found in England and France, and the spirit and efficiency he observed in Germany. Lindbergh was never pro-Nazi; he did not like Hitler's totalitarianism; and he was shocked by Nazi persecution of the Jews. He urged Britain, France, and the United States to step up their air-power preparations. By the late thirties, however, he believed that Britain and France were not capable of defeating Germany in war, that any attempt to do so would result in defeat, and that even if they could crush Germany the result would be such death and devastation that it could destroy western civilization. The only real victors in such a war, he feared, might be Japan and Communist Russia.[3]

In the spring of 1939, Lindbergh returned to the United States. At the request of Gen. H. H. Arnold, Colonel Lindbergh served five months with the Army Air Corps helping to speed American air-power preparations. With the beginning of the European war in September 1939, he decided that the greatest service he could perform for the United States would be to use his knowledge and influence to oppose American involvement in the war. It was not a task he enjoyed. But in those troubled times he considered it the most important service he could render. And he was prepared to endure the abuse his efforts were certain to bring him.

2. For the American military attaché's description of Lindbergh's role, *see* Colonel Truman Smith, "Air Intelligence Activities: Office of the Military Attaché, American Embassy, Berlin, Germany, August 1935–April 1939, with Special Reference to the Services of Colonel Charles A. Lindbergh, Air Corps (Res.)," 1956, Charles A. Lindbergh Papers, Sterling Memorial Library, Yale University, New Haven, Conn.; Lindbergh provided his own record of his experiences abroad in *The Wartime Journals of Charles A. Lindbergh* (New York: Harcourt Brace Jovanovich, 1970), pp. 3–178; Anne Morrow Lindbergh's account of those years is *The Flower and the Nettle: Diaries and Letters of Anne Morrow Lindbergh, 1936–1939* (New York and London: Harcourt Brace Jovanovich, 1976).

3. This summary of Colonel Lindbergh's views on developments in Europe is based on research in Lindbergh's letters written at that time and now in Sterling Memorial Library at Yale University; on Lindbergh's published *Wartime Journals;* on letters and accounts by individuals who knew Lindbergh closely; and on conversations and correspondence with General Lindbergh, 1972–1974.

For twenty-seven months before the Japanese attack on Pearl Harbor, Lindbergh was the most prominent, independent, and controversial opponent of American involvement in the war. He initiated his efforts in 1939 with nationwide broadcasts and with articles in popular magazines. In 1940, he began addressing public meetings. Early in 1941, he testified at Senate and House committee hearings in opposition to Roosevelt's lend-lease proposal. In April 1941, he joined the America First Committee, the leading noninterventionist pressure group, and became its most popular and controversial speaker.[4]

Colonel Lindbergh was never a pacifist, and he did not want to isolate the United States from the rest of the world. He called for "an independent destiny for America." He insisted that air power and geography strengthened America's defenses. In his words, "The air defense of America is as simple as the attack is difficult." Lindbergh had no confidence in Hitler's promises, but he believed that Germany could not successfully attack a prepared America. He opposed American aid to Britain, believing that it added to bloodshed abroad, would not change the course of the war there, and weakened American defenses at home. He favored a negotiated peace in Europe. When Nazi Germany attacked Communist Russia on 22 June 1941, Lindbergh saw the Russo-German war as one more reason America should not intervene. He urged the United States to prepare its military defenses, stay out of the European war, and perfect its own way of life at home.

Lindbergh repeatedly warned against propaganda by "powerful elements" that he believed were pressing the United States toward war. As America drew closer to involvement, he determined to name those groups that he thought were most responsible. He did so on 11 September 1941 in his most controversial address at an America First rally in Des Moines, Iowa. He correctly anticipated the damaging consequences it would have for him. In that speech he singled out some capitalists, anglophiles, intellectuals, and communists as "war agitators" of "lesser importance." But, he charged, "The three most important groups who have been pressing this country toward war are the British, the Jewish, and the Roosevelt Administration." The ensuing uproar focused largely on his reference to Jewish interventionists, but that was his only public mention of Jews. In contrast, during 1941 Lindbergh increasingly concentrated his attacks

---

4. Lindbergh's own account of his battle against intervention, 1939–1941, is in his published *Wartime Journals,* pp. 249–561.

on President Franklin D. Roosevelt. Charging Roosevelt with "government by subterfuge," Lindbergh called for "new leadership." He contended that Roosevelt was leading the country to war while professing to be working for peace, that the President's secrecy and deception were destroying democracy at home while trying to save democracy abroad.[5]

With the Japanese attack on Pearl Harbor, Lindbergh immediately ceased his noninterventionist activity and gave full support to America's war against the Axis. When the White House blocked his efforts to regain his Air Force commission, he served as a civilian with the Ford and United Aircraft companies in the testing, development, and production of bombers and fighters. In 1944, as a civilian technical representative for United Aircraft, the forty-two-year-old Lindbergh flew fifty combat missions in P-38 and Corsair fighters in the South Pacific, shooting down a Japanese plane in the process.[6]

Lindbergh was proud of his efforts to keep the United States out of World War II. He never retracted his views, and he expected ultimate vindication from history. Throughout the rest of his life he continued to believe that he had been right before Pearl Harbor, and that many of the fundamental crises of our own times could be traced to World War II and to America's involvement in that war.[7]

It is impossible to run controlled experiments to determine with certainty what might have happened if the United States had followed Lindbergh's guidance. Most people today believe that he was wrong. We cannot resolve the unanswerable question of who was most nearly right before Pearl Harbor, but perhaps in some respects Lindbergh was not as mistaken as is commonly believed. The terrifying successes of the German Luftwaffe in providing air support for the blitzkrieg as it crushed Poland, Denmark, Norway, Luxembourg, the Netherlands, Belgium, and France in 1939/1940 dramatized the accuracy of Lindbergh's evaluation of German tactical air power in Europe. He

---

5. This summary of the views Lindbergh advanced in his battle against intervention, 1939–1941, is based on the final drafts of the speeches he read that are in the Lindbergh Papers in Sterling Memorial Library; on the articles he published in those years; and on his testimony against lend-lease published by the Senate Foreign Relations Committee and by the House Foreign Affairs Committee in 1941.

6. Lindbergh's own account of his wartime experiences is in his published *Wartime Journals*, pp. 565–1000; and in Charles A. Lindbergh, *Of Flight and Life* (New York: Charles Scribner's Sons, 1948).

7. For Lindbergh's views on the subject in 1969, *see Wartime Journals*, p. xv.

overestimated German strategic air power. But the RAF Spitfires and Hurricanes might not have prevailed in the Battle of Britain had it not been for three variables that neither Lindbergh nor Roosevelt could fully have anticipated: radar, which enabled RAF fighters to be at the right places at the right times; "Ultra" and the Enigma decoding machine, which enabled British (and later American) leaders to know the contents of secret German communications in advance of military engagements; and Reich Marshal Hermann Goering's blunder in redirecting Luftwaffe attacks away from British airfields and factories to raids on London.[8] Even with the RAF triumphant in the skies over England, Churchill and Roosevelt surely were wrong if they seriously believed that Britain alone could have defeated Germany and Italy on the European continent relying only on American aid-short-of-war. And they were wrong if they believed that all-out-aid-short-of-war would not draw the United States fully into the conflagration eventually.

One must also include the Russo-German war in the calculations. From 22 June 1941, onward, Nazi Germany poured most of its strength into the awesome task of trying to defeat Communist Russia. Most of the more than 25 million who died in the European war were lost in eastern Europe. Without the Russo-German war, the power that Hitler could have brought to bear on the Western Wall would have been vastly greater than it was. The United States and Britain might have defeated Germany and Italy without Ultra and without the Russo-German war. Even Lindbergh did not rule out that possibility. But one must surely shudder at the consequences that such a so-called "victory" might have had for British and American lives, democracy, economy, and civilization. The answers to the question of the relative wisdom of alternative policies proposed before Pearl Harbor may not be so simple or clear-cut as "conventional wisdom" would have us believe.

Whatever one concludes on that question, Charles Lindbergh believed (as I

8. Winston S. Churchill, *The Second World War: Their Finest Hour* (Boston: Houghton Mifflin Co., 1949), pp. 319–43; F. W. Winterbotham, *The Ultra Secret* (New York: Harper & Row, 1974); Adolf Galland, *The First and the Last: The Rise and Fall of the German Fighter Forces, 1938–1945* (New York: Ballantine Books, 1954), pp. 10–38; Werner Baumbach, *The Life and Death of the Luftwaffe* (New York: Ballantine Books, 1960), pp. 79–87; Derek Wood and Derek Dempster, *The Narrow Margin: The Battle of Britain and the Rise of Air Power, 1930–1940* (New York: McGraw-Hill Book Co., 1961), pp. 21–31, 409–416; Francis K. Mason, *Battle over Britain* (London: McWhirter Twins Ltd., 1969), pp. 484–88.

do) that as a free citizen in a democratic country he had both the right and the duty to advance his views and to oppose through orderly processes those policies that he believed were dangerously unwise and unsound. But he was compelled to pay a high price for opposing American involvement. Attacks on Lindbergh began on a small scale in 1936 when he first visited Germany; they increased in October 1938, when Goering unexpectedly awarded him a medal at a dinner given by the United States ambassador to Germany; they grew more strident in September 1939, when he began speaking out against intervention; they reached ear-splitting levels in September 1941, after his Des Moines speech; and they have never really stopped. To some degree, a newer, urbanized, industrialized America was attacking values and perspectives of an older, simpler, more self-reliant rural and small-town America; Lindbergh personified foreign policy projections of the older America in its losing contest with the new. Lindbergh's assailants included the most vocal, literate, and powerful opinion-shaping elites. Attacks emanated from all the groups he named in his Des Moines speech. Newsmen continued their long feud with him. Attacks came from the White House, from Democrats who devotedly followed the President's leadership, and from President Roosevelt, himself.

Although 1977 marks the fiftieth anniversary of Lindbergh's flight across the Atlantic, it is also an anniversary of a different sort. Exactly thirty-seven years ago, President Roosevelt confided to his Secretary of the Treasury that he was "absolutely convinced that Lindbergh is a Nazi."[9] The very next day Roosevelt authorized his Attorney General to use wire taps "direct to the conversation or other communications of persons suspected of subversive activities."[10] Many letters to the White House supporting Lindbergh's views were turned over to the FBI and the Secret Service.[11] In April 1941, Roosevelt publicly compared Lindbergh to a copperhead, the term used for Northerners with pro-Southern

9. Henry Morgenthau, Jr., 20 May 1940, Presidential Diaries, p. 563, Franklin D. Roosevelt Papers, Hyde Park, N.Y.

10. Franklin D. Roosevelt, Confidential Memorandum to Attorney General, 21 May 1940, President's Secretary's File, Justice Department, Robert Jackson Folder, Franklin D. Roosevelt Papers, Hyde Park, N.Y.

11. Unsigned Memorandum, 31 May 1940, Official File 463-C, File Memo, 6 May 1941, Official File 4193, Franklin D. Roosevelt Papers, Hyde Park, N.Y.

12. Microfilm of Roosevelt's Press Conferences, 25 April 1941, roll 9, pp. 293–94; Lindbergh to Roosevelt, 28 April 1941, Official File 92, Franklin D. Roosevelt Papers, Hyde Park, N.Y.

sympathies during the Civil War. That attack led Colonel Lindbergh reluctantly to resign his Air Force commission.[12]

Even before Pearl Harbor, millions of Americans saw Lindbergh as little better than a Nazi. Similar to the guilt-by-association tactic that Senator Joseph McCarthy was to use a decade later, that image has persisted to our own day. Thirty years after Pearl Harbor when friends learned that I had had conversations with General Lindbergh and was doing research in his personal papers for a book on his opposition to the war, I got one of two different reactions. Some would brighten with interest and curiosity about the famous flyer. But others would respond with disdain. Their instant image of him was of a head-in-sand isolationist who at best was a naive dupe of the Nazis, or at worst was a conscious fascist dedicated to the triumph of Hitler's dictatorship.

Lindbergh fought with all the strength and ability he could command for a cause that he believed paramount for America and the world—and he lost. He suffered abuse and villification. But he tried to fight fairly, to focus on the issues, and to avoid *ad hominem* assaults. He rarely answered critics. Lindbergh's strength, independence, self-reliance, and courage made him less dependent on public approval than most might be. He said one must expect such attacks in public life. He went on to new challenges and accomplishments. Nonetheless, the attacks surely hurt him deeply, particularly when they came from those he respected and when his motives and views were distorted out of all recognition. Throughout his long ordeal, however, Lindbergh kept his sense of proportion, his integrity, and his pride.

It may be easy to seem heroic when the crowds are cheering; it surely must be difficult to be heroic when the crowds are screaming for one's head. The stigma from his battle against intervention outlived him. After his death, illustrators memorialized his passing with sketches of his *Spirit of St. Louis* winging off into eternity. But it might have been equally appropriate to have sketched that slender form standing straight and tall, bending his knee to no man, even when bloodied by the rocks that his assailants rained upon him.

Wayne S. Cole, professor of history at the University of Maryland, specializes in the history of American foreign relations. His Ph.D. is from the University of Wisconsin. He is the author of four books: *America First: The Battle against Intervention, 1940–1941* (1953, 1971); *Senator Gerald P. Nye and American Foreign Relations* (1962); *An Interpretive History of American Foreign Relations* (1968, 1974); and *Charles A. Lindbergh and the Battle against American Intervention in World War II* (1974). In 1962–1963 he was a Fulbright lecturer at the University of Keel in England. In 1973 he served as president of the Society for Historians of American Foreign Relations and also as a Fellow of the Woodrow Wilson International Center for Scholars.

His book on Lindbergh was based on extended personal conversations and correspondence with General Lindbergh, and on intensive reasearch into Lindbergh's letters and manuscripts at Yale University.

During World War II he was a flight instructor in the Army Air Forces. He has a commercial pilot certificate with an instrument rating and is a certified flight instructor. He has a total of 2,500 pilot hours.

Charles Lindbergh met Anne Morrow, daughter of the United States ambassador to Mexico, during a flying tour of Latin America sponsored by The Daniel Guggenheim Fund for the Promotion of Aeronautics. This photo of Anne Morrow Lindbergh was taken on a honeymoon cruise in June 1929.

Throughout the early 1930s, Charles and Anne Lindbergh pioneered airline routes around the world. In the fall of 1929, they accompanied Pan American Airways president Juan Trippe in inaugurating U.S. overseas air mail service in a Sikorsky flying boat.

The Sirius carried them to Nemuro, Japan, in August 1931 . . .

. . . and to Iceland in August 1933, where they met pioneer British pilot John Grierson (right).

Flying a Lockheed Sirius equipped with floats, Anne and Charles Lindbergh explored the routes that would one day be traveled by passenger airliners.

OVERLEAF

As technical consultant to TWA, Lindbergh played a major role in selecting the aircraft to be purchased by the firm. He is seen here entering the cockpit of a Northrup Alpha.

Lindbergh took serious interest in the technical advances pioneered by men like Igor Sikorsky

. . . and the dreams of the American astronautics pioneer, Robert Hutchings Goddard. Here he is seen with Goddard (center) and philanthropist Harry Guggenheim.

Anne and Charles Lindbergh were to spend the months from January 1936 to April 1939 in Europe. During a part of this time they lived in Illiec, an island off the coast of Brittany near the home of an old friend and colleague, Alexis Carrel, shown here with Lindbergh.

A Miles Mohawk, specially designed to meet Lindbergh's requirements, carried the pair on journeys around Europe and to points as far as Russia and India.

Ireland's Eamon de Valera was one of many European leaders the Lindberghs met during their years abroad. De Valera is shown here in 1936 clad in a flying suit borrowed from Lindbergh, at the site of the Shannon airport, near Limerick.

Lindbergh's most publicized visits during the European sojourn were his trips to Germany. These visits were made at the request of Maj. Truman Smith (background, smiling), a U.S. military attaché in charge of army and air intelligence in Berlin.

Lindbergh inspected German aircraft factories and studied the frightening growth of the Luftwaffe. He had an opportunity to speak with those who were shaping Nazi air policy . . .

. . . and others, like Hugo Eckener, the guiding spirit of German airship development, who opposed the course down which Adolf Hitler was leading the German nation.

He also had an opportunity to fly German military aircraft like this Ju 52.

Values of Flight and Life:
The Postwar Activities

JUDITH SCHIFF

In 1948, a generation away from the historic flight and its dazzling aftermath, Charles A. Lindbergh published a statement of his values in the form of a small book, *Of Flight and Life*. Lindbergh explained, "There are times in life when one feels an overwhelming desire to communicate belief to others, to band together with one's fellow-man in support of a common cause." He had felt such a desire on three occasions: when he "became convinced that man had a great destiny in the air" and devoted himself to building confidence in the "limitless future of the sky"; when he saw Europe preparing for war; and at that moment in the early cold war period when he stated,

I believe the values we are creating and the standards we are now following will lead to the end of our civilization, and that if we do not control our science by a higher moral force, it will destroy us with its materialistic values, its rocket aircraft, and its atom bombs.

Temporally, this statement was formulated halfway through Lindbergh's professional life. Throughout the remaining quarter-century he would often reevaluate, rework, and essentially reaffirm its basic premise. A new time for reappraisal began in 1941 when America's entrance into World War II ended Lindbergh's anti-intervention work.

After war was declared, Lindbergh immediately offered his services to the government. He was told that he could not regain his Air Force commission without publicly retracting his earlier views. Lindbergh then offered his services to the aviation industry, but the White House disapproved. The government did not stand in the way of Henry Ford's offer however, and at the age of thirty-nine, Lindbergh joined the Ford Motor Company working on the production of B-24 bombers at the Willow Run plant. Here, he observed daily the stultify-ing effect of the assembly line on the quality of life. To test the effect of high-altitude flying on pilots, he used himself as a guinea pig in an altitude chamber at the Aero Medical Unit of the Mayo Clinic. One day in actual test flying Lindbergh nearly lost his life when his oxygen supply ran out. Afterwards he reflected that "returning from the border of death always makes one more aware of life."

"To live," wrote Lindbergh in *Of Flight and Life,* "man needs both science and religion." The first need, science, Lindbergh learned to appreciate during flying missions in the South Pacific in the summer of 1944. After working with Ford, Lindbergh was able to contribute to the improvement of his first aviation love —the fighter plane. As a technical representative of United Aircraft, Lindbergh went to the South Pacific to instruct pilots in improved fuel economy. He had learned these techniques in his early flying days and practiced them on the New York to Paris flight. The young pilots were primarily concerned with speed and power and were untrained in fuel economy. Lindbergh personally demonstrated the value of these techniques by flying fifty combat missions. He returned each time with more fuel in reserve than the other pilots, and they gradually and cautiously followed his teaching. Pilots were then able to fly their P-38s 180 miles farther, reaching more distant targets.

One day, returning from a raid on the Japanese islands of Palau, Lindbergh was nearly shot down by a Japanese Zero. He was saved by the teamwork of his fellow pilots and their superior equipment. Lindbergh believed that without America's highly developed science, the war could not have been won. His South Pacific experiences, he felt, had taught him that "without a highly developed science, modern man lacks the power to survive."

The following year, just six days after Germany's surrender, Lindbergh again flew the Atlantic as consultant to the Naval Technical Mission in Europe, this time to study enemy developments in military aircraft and missiles. Observations of wartorn cities, the effects of the holocaust at Camp Dora, a branch of the concentration camp at Belsen, and the V-2 rocket production line, blasted out of solid rock and secreted in mountain tunnels at Nordhausen were manifestations of science gone haywire. Lindbergh felt that the Germans "had worshipped science": "To it they have sacrificed the quality of life—yet they have not gained the power to survive." He concluded that perhaps "survival in the last analysis was fully as dependent on the quality of life as in the power of arms—dependent on a perpetual balance of spiritual and material forces." What he learned in Germany, said Lindbergh, was that "if his civilization is to continue, modern man must direct the material power of his science by the spiritual truths of his God."

Lindbergh's work in the years following the war involved him principally in science and national security. In 1945 he worked with Army Ordnance at the University of Chicago in a secret project called CHORE (Chicago Ordnance Research). At the request of Secretary of the Air Force Stuart Symington and Gens. Hoyt Vandenberg and Lauris Norstad, Lindbergh became a consultant to the Air Force, to study ways of increasing the combat efficiency of the Strategic Air Command. As consultant he served on many boards and missions, including air base inspections and the operation of the Berlin Airlift. Twenty years after Charles and Anne Lindbergh flew "North to the Orient" in 1931, Lindbergh circled the North Pole in a four-engine Air Force reconnaissance plane. Despite the great advances made in a generation of aviation, Lindbergh commented on observing the frozen wasteland that "it seemed impossible that such a wilderness might be turned into a highway for assaulting forces of the future."

Lindbergh also flew with the 509th Atomic Bomb Group out of Walker Air Force Base, New Mexico. As part of the rigorous training in preparation for attack, they flew sixteen- to twenty-hour missions out of Labrador. While training for possible Russian attacks, Lindbergh was reminded of his three visits to Russia in 1931, 1935, and 1938. Although he had admired many of their accomplishments, what lingered in his mind was the obvious lack of freedom that marked the expressions and behavior of many Russian people.

Increasingly, Lindbergh felt the burden of seemingly endless planning projects. Sitting in hidden, windowless boardrooms, he felt more and more separated from life. For seven years he served on scientific committees charged with the development of ballistic missiles, especially those of intercontinental range. During the war, Lindbergh had valued the strength of arms in order to maintain freedom. He had experienced a sense of freedom of action even in combat, in the interaction of individuality and teamwork employed on flying missions. His youthful dreams of being a "Scout" pilot during World War I were finally realized in life-or-death air duels over the Pacific. But working with ballistic missiles gave him no sense of freedom. Lindbergh's fundamental concepts were now shaken. "I was faced with the dilemma," wrote Lindbergh " that our security today and tomorrow apparently required the production of weapons that were likely to destroy us the day after." Furthermore, he felt that the massive security systems "consume a fantastic amount of energy, and enslave us to the supply of oil, coal, and other irreplaceable natural resources of the earth."

In 1954, Lindbergh's wartime service was officially recognized when he was recommissioned and promoted by President Eisenhower to the rank of brigadier general. In citing his contributions, Eisenhower observed that Lindbergh's work had significantly shortened the war in the Pacific by enabling pilots to reach many targets formerly beyond their range.

At the same time, he was serving as a consultant to Pan American World Airways and traveled frequently over its far-flung routes. In the fifties and early sixties, he was dismayed by the rapid standardization he observed almost everywhere. On flights to Latin America in the twenties and to Europe, the Orient, Africa, and India in the thirties, Lindbergh had been fascinated with the beauty and variety of culture at every stop. The communication he had helped to promote was having a far different effect than he had envisioned.

Lindbergh again reassessed his priorities and concluded that the earth was more immediately threatened by mankind's lifestyle than by the possibility of total warfare. He announced his new priorities in a *Reader's Digest* article in 1964, in which he said that "the construction of an airplane is simple when compared to the evolutionary achievement of a bird: that airplanes depend upon an advanced civilization, and that where civilization is most advanced, few birds exist. I realized, that if I have to choose, I would rather have birds than airplanes."

During the last ten years of his life, he increasingly devoted his energies to conservation projects. Lindbergh traveled tirelessly to talk to heads of state about their endangered species: the whale, the monkey-eating eagle, the tamarau, the rhinoceros, and the polar bear. He enjoyed visiting and living with primitive tribes, many of whose values he preferred to those of modern civilization. The conservation groups to which he gave active support included the World Wildlife Fund, the International Union for the Conservation of Nature and Natural Resources, and Panamin (Private Association for National Minorities). Through Panamin, Lindbergh was able to visit and interact with the gentle Tasaday, a Stone Age tribe living in a Philippine rainforest. Observing man "shorn of his civilized accoutrements," Lindbergh felt that both he and the Tasaday were striving to reach a balance between the civilized and the primitive.

At home, Lindbergh began to speak out publicly for the first time since 1941. He addressed the Alaska legislature and the National Institute of Social Science, opposed the use of the supersonic transport plane on ecological and economic grounds and supported the work of the Congressional Subcommittee on Science, Research, and Development. In 1970, Lindbergh wrote to Congressman Daddario that he was becoming "constantly more impressed with the wisdom of" the committee's "new approach to scientific research and development through consideration of its effect on the future welfare of mankind." Lindbergh's contributions were recognized when he was awarded the Baruch Conservation Prize for 1968 and was honored by the National Institute of Sciences.

Lindbergh also devoted a good deal of his time to his writings. As early as 1938, he had begun to write his autobiography, but his first priority was to write a more thoughtful account of the flight and his early life. The hastily written *We*, which he had sandwiched in between postflight receptions and his U.S. tour, had not conveyed all that he wished of his early values. Just before taking off for Paris, Lindbergh, having spent most of the money provided by his backers, had signed a contract in New York to write a book with the help of an editor, based on the presumed success of the flight. Upon his return, he was presented with a ghostwritten product based on his newspaper stories, which dissatisfied him. Despite his lack of time and writing experience, he resolved to write the book himself. In less than a month he had finished *We*, which was a best seller for two years. Later that year, Lindbergh explained to his lawyer, "I have had several requests to sign statements and articles written by someone else. I have refused to sign anything I do not write, as I believe that if it is worth signing it is also worth writing."

In the early fifties, Lindbergh finally had the time to reflect on and relive those early experiences in writing *The Spirit of St. Louis*. Written in the historical present tense, it vividly transmits with the use of flashbacks, the excitement and joy of Lindbergh's adventures. Following is the record of his feelings just before testing the *Spirit of St. Louis* on 28 April 1927:

> *What a beautiful machine it is, resting there on the field in front of the hangar, trim and slender, gleaming in its silver coat! All our ideas, all our calculations, all our hopes lie there before me, waiting to undergo the acid test of flight. For me, it seems to contain the whole future of aviation. When such planes can be built, there's no limitation to the air.*

His literary genius was recognized in 1954 when he was awarded the 1953 Pulitzer Prize for autobiography and biography.

Thereafter, Lindbergh worked on the drafting of a complete autobiography. He proceeded slowly and thoughtfully, finding the writing process itself valuable as a method of analyzing his past thoughts and actions and as a guide for the future. Frequently he interrupted his writing to work on smaller projects, book forewords, and articles on conservation such as "The Wisdom of Wildness," "Lessons from the Primitive," and "Feel the Earth." Twenty-five years after the end of World War II, Lindbergh published his private wartime journals. The published version of the stacks of small, handwritten diaries covering the period 1938 through 1945 is over 1,000 pages. It was Lindbergh's hope in making his detailed documentary record readily available to the public that issues and conditions of the past would be clarified, "and thereby contribute to under-standing issues and conditions of the present and the future."

In writing what he eventually named the *Autobiography of Values,* Lindbergh was motivated to analyze the origins of his values. In the fall of 1969, he visited the Lindbergh homestead in Little Falls, Minnesota, in connection with the restoration project being carried out by the Minnesota Historical Society. (Since 1944, the Lindberghs had lived in Connecticut where their five children born between 1932 and 1945 grew up.) At the request of the director of the society, Russell W. Fridley, Lindbergh prepared reminiscences of his Minnesota boy-hood. The series of letters mailed from many parts of the world amounted to eighty-five pages and was compiled into a book, *Boyhood on the Upper Mississippi,* published in 1972.

Lindbergh made additional visits to the farm in 1970 and 1971. One of the last public occasions he attended was the dedication of the Interpretive Center at the Lindbergh home in the fall of 1973. In concluding his public address, Lindbergh reaffirmed his belief in nature as the primary value of man's existence:

> On this riverbank one can look upward in late evening and watch a satellite penetrate through stars, thereby spanning human progress from the primitive hunter with his canoe to the latest advance of our civilization. . . . I believe our civilization's latest advance is symbolized by the park rather than by satellite and space travel. In establishing parks and nature reserves, man reaches beyond the material values of science and technology. He recognizes the essential value of life itself, of life's natural inheritance irreplaceably evolved through earthly epochs, of the miraculous spiritual awareness that only nature in balance can maintain.

A visitor to Little Falls today can readily experience vicariously Lindbergh's boyhood in America's heartland. The town has changed little during this century. Congressman Lindbergh's law office building is still standing on the main intersection, and by the falls is the little Victorian Gothic railroad station where Lindbergh's mother arrived in 1900 as the new high school teacher from

Detroit. North of town stands the old water tower that young Lindbergh climbed to overcome his early fear of height. The town's close resemblance to the Gopher Prairie of Sinclair Lewis's *Main Street* is not surprising — Lewis's home town, Sauk Centre, is in the next county. Lindbergh's grandfather, August Lindbergh, a Swedish immigrant, settled just outside Sauk Centre in 1859 and in its sawmill suffered the accident that tore off his arm.

The Lindbergh farm, now a state park, is on the west bank below the falls. There one enters a completely different environment of woodland, wildlife, and sparkling blue water. Young Charles's favorite place was the back porch on a high bluff overlooking the Mississippi. He usually slept there, occasionally even in winter, warmed by piles of quilts and his dog. The view of tall tree tops at eye level amid sparkling stars as he drifted off to sleep remained in his mind's eye, and he associated it with his first dreams of flying. These dreams were intensified when Lindbergh attended his first air meet outside Washington, D.C., at Fort Myer, in 1912. Here Lindbergh saw mock air battles in which pioneer air aces, or aeronauts, as they were called, threw oranges at ground targets. Unfortunately, he would have to wait yet another ten years before experiencing his first flight. A few years before an airplane had flown over the farm and stimulated his dream of reaching the stars. On 9 April 1922, Lindbergh's dream was realized in Lincoln, Nebraska, where he took his first flight. Reflecting on those early flying experiences in his yet unpublished autobiography, Lindbergh writes:

> *The life of an aviator seemed to me ideal. It involved skill. It brought adventure. It made use of the latest developments of science. . . . Mechanical engineers were fettered to factories and drafting boards while pilots have the freedom of wind with the expanse of sky. There were times in an airplane when it seemed I had partially escaped mortality to look down on earth like a God.*

In looking back on his life, Lindbergh evaluated the major formative influences. From his parents he had learned to love both nature and science. For many years, science and technology absorbed most of his attention. In growing up, his grandfather, Charles Land, had also been a strong influence. Dr. Land, a pioneer dentist and inventor, had lost his fortune and reputation through his dedication to his scientific work, as did Lindbergh's father and grandfather Lindbergh through their dedication to liberal political beliefs. Then, in falling in love and marrying Anne Morrow, Lindbergh was influenced by a new world of society and culture. In the thirties, his scientific values were enriched when he came to know Robert Goddard, the father of modern rocketry, and Alexis Carrel, the Nobel Prize–winning biologist with whom he collaborated in tissue culture experiments.

In the sixties, long after Lindbergh's experiments were halted by the war and then by Carrel's death, medical researchers at the U. S. Naval Medical Institute continued his work. In 1966, Lindbergh and several colleagues published an article in the journal *Cryobiology,* which reported improvements in maintaining organs removed from large animals. These experiments would further attempts to freeze whole organs successfully for transplantation. Lindbergh's contribution was the enlargement and improvement with new plastic materials of the pulsating perfusion pump he had developed thirty years earlier. His belief in simplicity, which had characterized the success of the transatlantic flight, also marked his scientific work. In a letter to Lindbergh, a colleague wrote, "There have been many attempts with much more elaborate equipment to extend your reported studies but of the more recent efforts none have succeeded in long term functional organ preservation. . . . Your results far exceed the best studies with the newer techniques." At this time, the Corning Glass Company began to produce perfusion pumps of Lindbergh's design.

In the field of rocket technology, Lindbergh marvelled at the changes that had taken place since he had inspected Goddard's rocket launching tower (converted from a windmill) in Roswell, New Mexico, in 1936. Then the slender fifteen-foot rocket had been transported to the stand on the back of a small pickup truck. In December 1968, Lindbergh witnessed the launching of the Apollo 8 flight around the moon. Afterward, when asked to write an article for *Life* magazine assessing the astronauts' mission, he declined. His lengthy and thoughtful letter of explanation so impressed the editor that he asked to publish it. In this frank statement written forty-two years after the transatlantic flight, Lindbergh assessed his changing values of flight and life. He wrote he had been "hypnotized by the launching" in whose "flashing, billowing chaos," he "shook with the earth itself." "For a moment," continued Lindbergh, "reality and memory contorted, and Robert Goddard stood watching at my side. Was he now the dream; his dream, the reality?"

At that moment, Lindbergh explained, he felt an "almost overwhelming desire to reenter the fields of astronautics." But he would not because "decades spent in contact with science and its vehicles" had directed his "mind and senses to an area beyond their reach." "Following the paths of science," he wrote, "we become constantly more aware of mysteries beyond scientific research. In these vaguely apprehended azimuths, I think the great adventures of the future lie in voyages inconceivable by our twentieth century rationality." Lindbergh believed that "early entrance to this era can be attained by the application of our scientific knowledge not to life's mechanical vehicles but to the essence of life itself." Upon such application depended the survival of mankind. "That is why," concluded Lindbergh, "I have turned my attention from technological progress to life, from the civilized to the wild."

Again reflecting late in life on his early values, Lindbergh determined in his autobiography what drew him to aviation:

When I look back on early years, I realize it was the art of flying more than its science that intrigued me — it was the combination of an underdeveloped science with an art, resulting in adventure for the mind and body that brought stimulation to the spirit. As the science has developed, the art and adventure have declined — and with them, has my interest.

During the last two years of his life, Lindbergh strove to complete the final statement of his values from the vast collection of his papers that he had been placing in the Yale University Library since 1941. He consulted his letters, diaries, flying logs, photographs, special subject files, and ephemera, as well as the voluminous pages of notes compiled over the years, which he headed "Incidents of Memory and for Further Thought." Literary fragments set down over the years include observations on the deteriorating condition of the earth as seen from the air, reminiscences, and guidelines for actions and the writing of his autobiography. "Life is like a landscape," he wrote in one notation: "You live in the midst of it, but can describe it only from the vantage point of distance." In writing, Lindbergh studied himself objectively and subjectively and carefully recorded his conclusions. As he had performed countless scientific experiments in the thirties, he retested his values and beliefs in written revisions. His *Autobiography of Values* is his legacy to mankind.

Just before his final flight to Hawaii, two weeks before his death on 26 August 1974, Charles Lindbergh turned over to his friend and publisher, William Jovanovich, an uncompleted manuscript of over 1,000 typed pages and several times that number of pages of related notes. For the past two years, William

Jovanovich and I have been editing the autobiography for publication. The last dated writing among the notes is a poetic statement of 20 June 1974, which provides a fitting epitaph.

I turn again to my microscope's bleak, parched, dry, and lifeless field
  As those cells disappeared, so will I
    Tens of millions of men die yearly
But in how many ways will I continue to exist
  In my children, in my lifestream, in memories,
                              on printed pages,
        in my impact on environment
What of my molecular and atomic being?
  Molecules that have taken part in structure and
                              in training,
    countless trillions. After death, others
    return to life and air.
  What memories and intelligences do they retain?
  Molecules transfer from animals & food to me,
    and from me back to animals & food — enter
    & return from air and sky.
    They came from stars, so I am of stars.
    Messages from the stars are absorbed by my
    eye at night — and returned in thought.
Time: Long? short?
    Now man, now leaf —
    The form of man is everything. What else is the form of God?

Charles A. Lindbergh, *Of Flight and Life* (New York: Charles Scribner's Sons, 1948); *The Spirit of St. Louis* (New York: Charles Scribner's Sons, 1953); *The Wartime Journals of Charles A. Lindbergh* (New York: Harcourt Brace Jovanovich, 1970); and materials drawn from the Charles Lindbergh Papers, Sterling Memorial Library, Yale University, were consulted during the preparation of this paper.

JUDITH ANN SCHIFF, chief research archivist, Yale University Library, has enjoyed a long association with the Lindberghs. Since her appointment as librarian of historical manuscripts in 1963, she has administered their collected papers and assisted in the preparation of several of their books, including *The Wartime Journals of Charles A. Lindbergh* and the *Diaries and Letters of Anne Morrow Lindbergh*.

Schiff is immediate past president of New England Archivists, a director of the Association for the Study of Connecticut History, and associate editor of their *Journal*. She is also president of the League of Women Voters of New Haven.

For the past two years, she has been editing, with William Jovanovich, the unfinished autobiography of Charles Lindbergh and recently published two articles relating to Lindbergh —"The Life and Letters of Charles A. Lindbergh: A Commemorative View" in the *Yale Library Gazette* and "The Literary Lindbergh Is Celebrated at Yale," an account of her editing experiences published in the *Yale Alumni Magazine*. Lindbergh's final statement, *The Autobiography of Values*, will be published by Harcourt Brace Jovanovich in January 1978.

Technical Preparation of the Airplane "Spirit of St. Louis"

TECHNICAL NOTES
NATIONAL ADVISORY COMMITTEE FOR AERONAUTICS

No. 257

Written for the National Advisory Committee for Aeronautics

By

DONALD A. HALL
Chief Engineer, Ryan Airlines, Inc.

Washington

July 1927

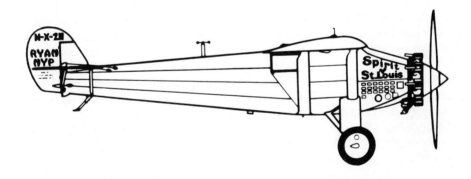

It would be impossible to provide a proper commemoration of the fiftieth anniversary of the first transatlantic air crossing without devoting some attention to the immortal *Spirit of St. Louis*. The following paper, "Technical Preparation of the *Spirit of St. Louis*," was originally published in 1927 as Technical Note No. 257 of the National Advisory Committee for Aeronautics. The author, Donald A. Hall, was chief engineer with Ryan Airlines and had primary responsibility for the design of the airplane.

In order to clarify the current impressions as to the technical preparation, in connection with both the design and performance, of the airplane used by Colonel Charles A. Lindbergh, the following information is presented.

The development of this airplane was begun with the idea of using a standard model Ryan M-2 and making modifications to suit the special purpose. Upon Colonel Lindbergh's arrival at the factory, it was quickly determined that modification of the M-2 was less practicable than redesign. Colonel Lindbergh laid out the following basic specifications: That the airplane should be a monoplane type, powered with a single Wright J5C engine, have a good power reserve on take-off when carrying more than 400 gallons of gasoline and must have the pilot located in rear of all tanks for safety in a forced landing.

The decision on these basic specifications immediately determined the inadvisability of using the standard Ryan M-2 model. The airplane was then laid out anew, the fuselage following the standard model approximately in regard to design and structure, but being lengthened by 2 feet. The fuselage structure was redesigned to suitable load factors in flight and landing with full load. A wide tread split axle chassis was designed to a four load factor at full designed load. The wing structure was designed to suitable load factors in high incidence, low incidence, and diving conditions at full designed load.

At this point Colonel Lindbergh began to take a very active interest in the design of the airplane, and until the airplane had completed its flight tests he closely cooperated with the engineering department of the Ryan Company. The location of the pilot's cockpit (cabin) in the rear of the fuselage and entirely enclosed, which is the most radical feature of the design, had its development based on the primary requisite of safety, it being considered that in the event of an accident the pilot would be in the safest position in which it would be possible to be placed.

The periscope was suggested by Mr. Randolph, of the Ryan Airlines, who had had considerable submarine experience. This suggestion was accepted by Colonel Lindbergh with the limitation that if it was not satisfactory or was of any aerodynamical disadvantage it would be discarded at New York. The periscope consisted of a panel in the instrument board through which a view directly to the front was afforded by an angular mirror, having a frontal size of about 3 by 5 inches, which projected from the left side of the fuselage, and which could be retracted when not in use. The device proved of no disadvantage aerodynamically on account of the retractable feature, and was of certain utility during the flights of the airplane.

The engine, to ensure proper balance, was of necessity moved forward considerably. The additional space in the forward part of fuselage which was provided by this extension was utilized for the oil tank, located directly in the rear of the engine and a gasoline tank in the rear of the oil tank. The oil and tank provided an excellent fire wall. It was found that with full load the two tanks, although so far forward, did not interfere with the trim of the airplane to an extent which could not readily be taken care of by the adjustable stabilizer.

All of the various items of design had very careful consideration, in which Colonel Lindbergh took a prominent part. The interest shown by him in the detailed design and construction of the airplane was in no way a critical interest.

Colonel Lindbergh's time was further occupied during the period in which the airplane was under construction in a careful and intensive study of navigation. This study was most complete. During four weeks practically all his waking hours were occupied by this study of navigation and the preparation of charts and data for use in a dead reckoning flight. It should be borne in mind that he had practically no technical knowledge of the art of navigation prior to this time with the exception of such aerial navigation as he had had in his Army and Air Mail experience.

Members of the Ryan Airlines factory organization who were responsible for the construction of the airplane are Mr. B. F. Mahoney, President of the Company; Mr. W. H. Bowlus, Factory Manager; Mr. Bert Tindale, Shop Superintendent, and in charge of wing department; Mr. Walter Locke, in charge of Purchasing Department, who also assisted in engineering; Mr. McNeal, in charge of Final Assembly Department; Mr. Fred Rohr, in charge of Tank and Cowling Department; Mr. Fred Ayers, in charge of Covering and Finishing Department; Mr. Anderson, in charge of Welding Department; Mr. Morrow, in charge of Fitting Department, in addition to the writer.

Colonel Lindbergh paid close attention to the final assembly securing a thorough practical knowledge of the major units, especially the fuel system.

Immediately upon the completion of assembly, the flight tests were begun, the preparation for which had been made in detail. Colonel Lindbergh had laid out with the writer the tests to be made, and all of the test flights were flown by Colonel Lindbergh himself, who is the only pilot who has ever flown this airplane.

A program of tests were carried out which was sufficiently comprehensive to check the theoretical performance. A series of flights with fuel loads of from 36 to 300 gallons was made for the specific purpose of checking take-off distances.

All of these flight tests were made for the primary purpose of checking the theoretical figures as to performance, and while not as comprehensive as might have been possible had more time been available, were sufficient in the opinion of Colonel Lindbergh.

It is hoped that from these few paragraphs it will be understood that the ultimate performance of the *Spirit of St. Louis* is largely the result of the exceptionally careful and painstaking effort on the part of Colonel Lindbergh in his preparations while at San Diego, and that his evident confidence in the Ryan Airline organization was merited. It is the belief of the writer that Colonel Lindbergh did not leave San Diego until he was absolutely certain that he had an airplane with which the transatlantic flight was possible, and that this conclusion was reached after a tremendous volume of work which he set for himself and accomplished while at the Ryan Airlines factory.

MODIFICATIONS OF CONSTRUCTION

In order to sustain the increased loads resulting from the full load required for the New York to Paris flight, it was necessary to increase the wing span by 10 feet and to redesign all the structural members of the wing cellule and fuselage. The wing ribs were more closely spaced (11 inches on centers) and plywood was fitted on the leading edge of the wing running from the top of the front spar around to the bottom of the spar. On account of the increased moment arm the ailerons were reduced in area and were located inboard from the wing tips. This was expected to reduce wing tip deflection and give better aerodynamic efficiency. The wing tips, in plan form, were given an airfoil contour.

To suit the increased wing span and for increased safety the landing gear was given a wider tread. Dual axles (front and rear integral) made of chrome molybdenum steel tubing heat-treated to 180,000 lb./sq. in., were used. The shock absorber was of trombone type with 8 individual links of cord and a 6½ inch rise.

The tail surfaces were practically the same as those of the M-2 but were installed 2 feet farther aft on the lengthened fuselage. The streamlining of the fuselage was entirely new and was worked out so that any longitudinal section of the fuselage gives a smooth curve from propeller spinner to tail. A fillet streamline was used at the junction of the bottom of the wing and the fuselage.

The tail skid was made of heat-treated chrome molybdenum steel tubing of the same quality as the axles.

The power plant consisted of a single Wright J5C engine, a stock model. The tanks for oil and gasoline were all of terneplate. The three wing gasoline tanks together had a capacity of 152 gallons, the center fuselage tank 210 gallons, and the forward fuselage tank 88 gallons. The designed gasoline capacity was 425 gallons. It came out 450 gallons.

All the gasoline tanks connected to a Lunkenheimer distributor in the pilot's cabin and it was possible to pump from any tank to any other. There were two fuel systems to the engine. In addition to the other instruments, an econometer invented by Colonel Lindbergh was used on the fuel system.

The 25-gallon oil tank was arranged between pilot and engine so as to act as a fire wall.

General Dimensions and Specifications of the Airplane Are as Follows:

GENERAL

Span .... 46 ft.

Chord .... 7 ft.

Wing area .... 319 sq. ft.

Airfoil .... Clark Y

Engine, Wright J5C, giving 223 bhp at 1800 rpm

Propeller, Standard Steel Propeller Co., dural. set at .... 16¼ pitch

WEIGHTS

Empty, complete with instruments 2,150 lb.

USEFUL LOAD

Pilot .... 170 lb.

Miscellaneous .... 40 lb.

Gasoline, 425 gal. (Western at 6.12 lb./gal.) .... 2,600 lb.

Oil, 25 gal. (at 7 lb./gal.) .... 175 lb.

2,985 lb.

Gross weight fully loaded at start of flight .... 5,135 lb.

Gross weight lightly loaded at end of flight without gasoline and food but with 10 gal. of oil left .... 2,415 lb.

LOADING

Wing loading:
(Full load at start of flight = 16.10 lb./sq. ft.)
(Light load at end of flight = 7.57 lb./sq. ft.)

Power loading:
(Full load at start of flight = 23.0 lb./bhp)
(Light load at end of flight = 10.8 lb./bhp)

CALCULATED PERFORMANCE (rpm data based on test and theory)

Maximum speed:
(Full load = 120.0 mph)
(Light load = 124.5 mph)

Minimum speed:
(Full load = 71 mph)
(Light load = 49 mph)

Economic speed:
(Full load = 97 mph at 1670 rpm)
(Light load = 67 mph at 1080 rpm)

FUEL ECONOMY AT ECONOMIC SPEEDS

Full load with full rich mixture = 6.95 mi./gal.

Light load with lean mixture = 13.9 mi./gal.

RANGE

At ideal speeds of 97 start and 67 mph at end = 4,110 mi.

At practical speeds of 95 start and 75 mph at end = 4,040 mi.

FLIGHT TEST PERFORMANCE

Maximum speed:
With 25 gal. gas & 5 gal. oil = 129 mph over 3 km course

With full load of 425 gal. gas & 25 gal. oil = 124 mph approximate based on calculated performance.

With 25 gal. gas & 4 gal. oil by air-speed meter = 128 mph

With 201 gal. gas & 4 gal. oil by air-speed meter = 127 mph

TAKE-OFF DISTANCES

Tests made at Camp Kearney near San Diego, Calif., at 600 ft. altitude. Oil = 4 gal.

Gas gal.	Gross Wt. lb.	Approx. Head Wind Velocity mph	Take-off Distance ft.
36	2,600	7	229
71	2,800	9	287
111	3,050	9	389
151	3,300	6	483
201	3,600	4	615
251	3,900	2	800
301	4,200	0	1,023

Weight Characteristics When Ryan NYP Left New York

Empty complete with tanks and instruments .... 2,150 lb.

USEFUL LOAD

Pilot .... 170 lb.

Miscellaneous .... 40 lb.

Gas 450 gal.
(California at 6.12 lb./gal.) .... 2,750 lb.

Oil, 20 gal. at 7 lb./gal. .... 140 lb.

3,1000 lb.

GROSS WEIGHT

Fully loaded (25 gal. gas over design
load) .... 5,250 lb.

NET EMPTY WEIGHT

Empty weight of 2,150 lb. includes all tanks
and special equipment and instruments.

Assuming a gas capacity of 60 gallons and oil
of 5 gallons sufficient for ordinary flying, the

weight of excess tanks and special equipment
and instruments equals 450 lb.

Net empty weight = 2,150−450 = 1,700 lb.

TOTAL USEFUL LOAD

Total useful load   = 5,250−1700 = 3,550 lb.

RATIO OF WEIGHTS

Ratio of useful load to gross weight = .68

Gross weight = 3.1 times net empty weight.

LOADING
(Fully loaded)

Wing loading = 16.5 lb./sq. ft.

Power loading = 23.6 lb./bhp (223 bhp at
1,800 rpm).

Airplane structure designed to suitable load
factors at full design load.

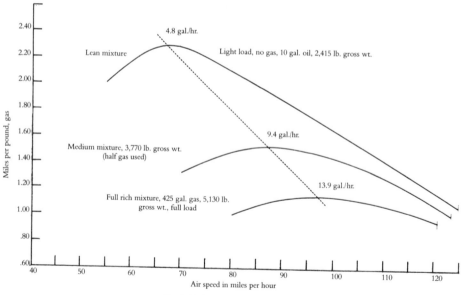

Fig. 1   Fuel economy, Ryan NYP airplane

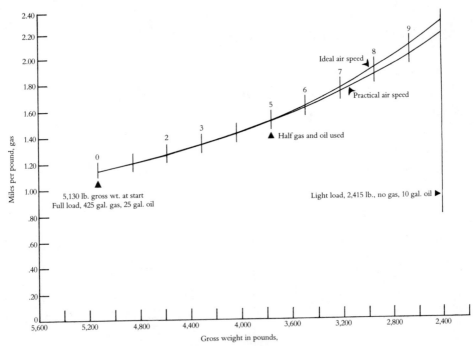

Fig. 2 Ryan NYP airplane.

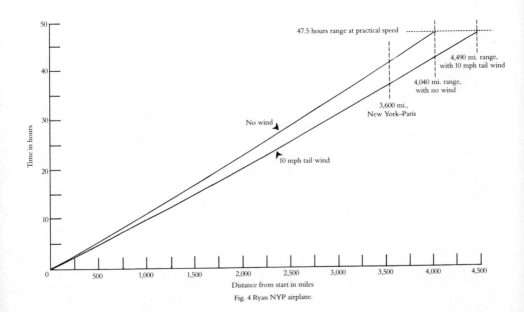

Fig. 4 Ryan NYP airplane.

Man Hours to Build Ryan NYP Airplane

CONSTRUCTION

3,000 man hours to build not including superintendent's and manager's time.

ENGINEERING

775 hours by designer, including performance calculations and flight testing.

75 hours put in by men in other departments (man hours).

850 man hours total engineering time between February 26 and May 10, when NYP left San Diego for Saint Louis.

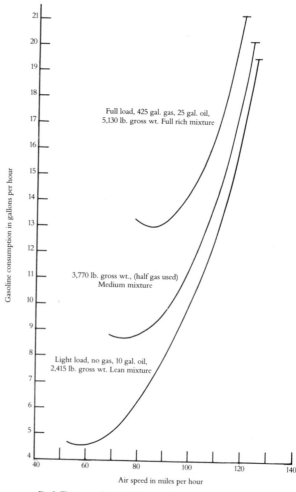

Full load, 425 gal. gas, 25 gal. oil, 5,130 lb. gross wt. Full rich mixture

3,770 lb. gross wt., (half gas used) Medium mixture

Light load, no gas, 10 gal. oil, 2,415 lb. gross wt. Lean mixture

Gasoline consumption in gallons per hour

Air speed in miles per hour

Fig. 3 Western gasoline at 6.12 lb./gal. weight used, Ryan NYP airplane.

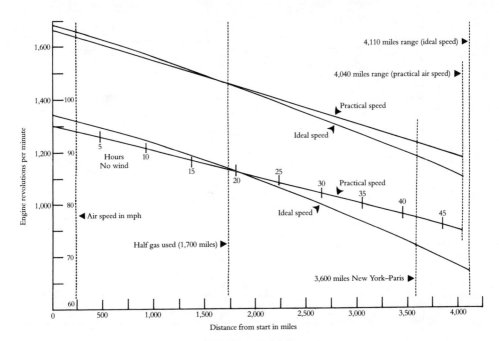

Fig. 5 Ryan NYP airplane.

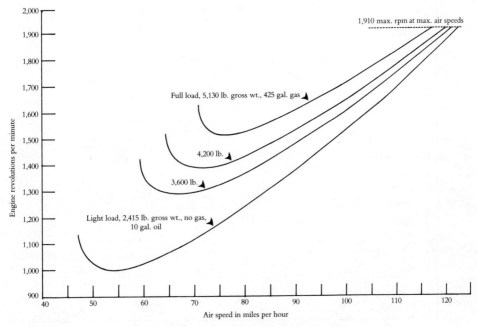

Fig. 6 Based on flight tests and experimental theory, Ryan NYP airplane.

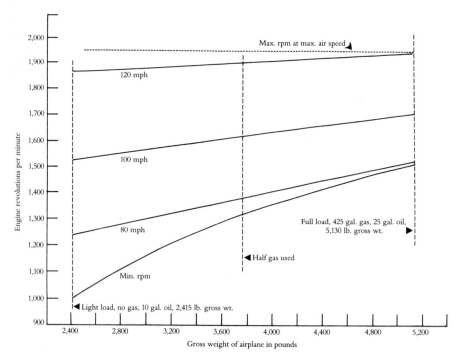

Fig. 7 Ryan NYP airplane.

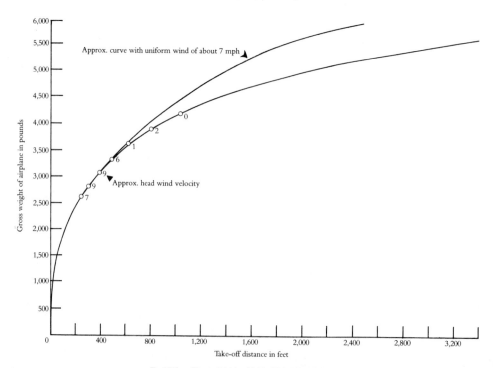

Fig. 8 Take-off tests. Altitude of field, 600 ft. Ryan NYP airplane.

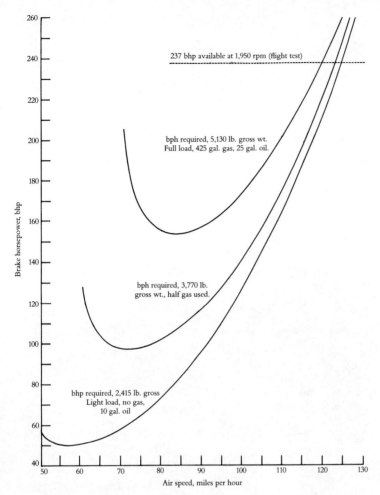

Fig. 9 Ryan NYP airplane.

260

240 — 237 bhp available at 1,950 rpm (flight test)

220

200   bph required, 5,130 lb. gross wt.
                Full load, 425 gal. gas, 25 gal. oil.

180

160

Brake horsepower, bhp

140

120   bph required, 3,770 lb.
         gross wt., half gas used.

100

80   bhp required, 2,415 lb. gross
        Light load, no gas,
          10 gal. oil

60

40
50   60   70   80   90   100   110   120   130
Air speed, miles per hour

During World War II, Lindbergh was sent to the Pacific, where he demonstrated the combat potential of the F4U Corsair in combat and taught pilots to increase the range of their P-38 fighters by paying careful attention to fuel settings.

Following World War II, Lindbergh served on various official boards and commissions, including the Air Force Academy Site Selection Board.

He also maintained his contact with the aircraft industry and airlines, as in this photo of the Falcon Jet board of directors taken at the Paris Air Show in 1973.

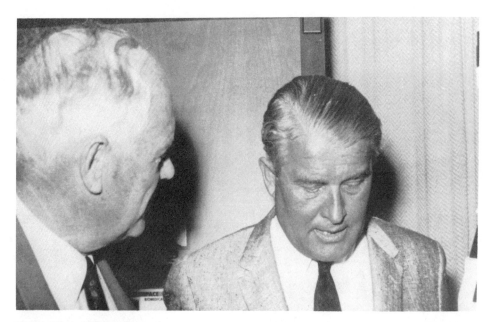

Lindbergh watched in fascination as the dream of Robert Goddard was transformed into reality. He is shown here with Wernher von Braun during a reception at the time of the Apollo 11 launch, 15 July 1969. (Photo Mitchell R. Sharpe)

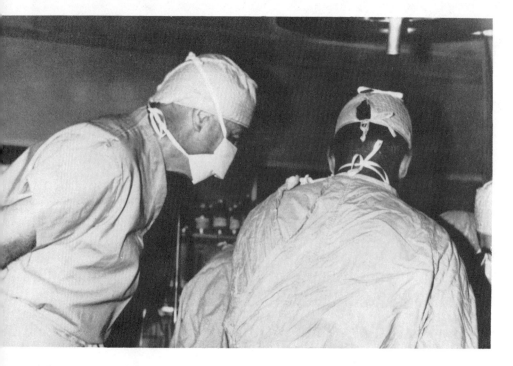

Lindbergh's early collaboration with Alexis Carrel on the development of the perfusion pump led to a continuing interest in medical technology. He is seen here with surgeon Denton A. Cooley in 1967.

Lindbergh became increasingly interested in the impact of the technology on the natural environment. He participated in a number of major expeditions to study the inhabitants and wildlife of remote areas. This photo was taken during an Indonesian trip in 1967...

OVERLEAF
...and this the following year on a trip to Baja, California.

His affection for the Tasaday people of Mindinao and his desire to protect their simple lifestyle from encroachments by the modern world were central concerns of Lindbergh's later years.

A Selected Bibliography

DOMINICK A. PISANO

The compiler wishes to acknowledge the efforts of previous researchers, without whose work the present compilation would not have been possible. Among these are Arthur G. Renstrom, former head of the Aeronautics Section, Science and Technology Division, Library of Congress, whose comprehensive bibliography appeared in consecutive issues of the *Library of Congress Information Bulletin* for 13 May and 20 May, 1977; and Kenneth S. Davis and Walter S. Ross for their diligent work in uncovering the bibliographic data that appeared in their respective biographies of Charles A. Lindbergh, *The Hero: Charles A. Lindbergh and the American Dream* (Garden City, N.Y.: Doubleday & Co., 1959) and *The Last Hero: Charles A. Lindbergh* (New York: Harper & Row, 1976).

SELECTED WRITINGS OF CHARLES A. LINDBERGH

Notice by Cadet Charles A. Lindbergh of Parachute Jump Made at Kelly Field, Texas, 6 March 1925, *Air Service News Letter* 6, (12 April 1925): 6–7.

"Going over the Side Three Times with a Parachute." *U. S. Air Services* (February 1927): 42–43.

"And Then I Jumped." *Saturday Evening Post* (23 July 1927): 6–7.

"Report of Northbound Mail Flight, 3 November 1926, by Charles A. Lindbergh, Pilot, Contract Air Mail, No. 2." *Review of Reviews* (August 1927): 202–204.
Reprinted from the *U. S. Official Postal Guide, Monthly Supplement,* June 1927.

"The Making of an Air Mail Pilot: The Unforgettable Thrills of the First Solo Flight." *World's Work* (September 1927): 472–81.

We: The Famous Flier's Own Story of His Life and Transatlantic Flight, together with His Views on the Future of Aviation. Foreword by Myron T. Herrick. New York: G. P. Putnam's Sons, 1927.
Also published, New York: Grosset & Dunlap, 1927, by arrangement with G.P. Putnam's Sons. Excerpts appeared in "When 'Lucky Slim' Went a-Barnstorming," *Literary Digest* (13 August 1927): 34, 36, 38, 40.

"To Bogota and Back by Air." *National Geographic Magazine* (May 1928): 529–601.

National Education Association. Address on the Need for the Study and Teaching of Elementary Aeronautics in the American School System, *Proceedings of the 66th Annual Meeting Held at Minneapolis, Minnesota, July 1–6, 1928,* vol. 66. Minneapolis: n.p., 1928. pp. 808–809.

"Air Transport." *Saturday Evening Post* (1 February 1930): 7, 50.

"Method for Washing Corpuscles in Suspension." *Science* (15 April 1932): 415–16.

Foreword to "Flying around the North Atlantic," by Anne M. Lindbergh. *National Geographic Magazine* (September 1934): 259–337.

Maps to *North to the Orient,* by Anne M. Lindbergh. New York: Harcourt, Brace & Co., 1935.

Field notes and material to "Collecting Microörganisms from the Arctic Atmosphere," by F. C. Meier. *Scientific Monthly* (January 1935): 5–20.

"Aviation and War." *Vital Speeches of the Day* (1 August 1936): 696.
Delivered at a luncheon given in his honor by the German Air Ministry in Berlin, 23 July 1936.

Carrel, Alexis, and Lindbergh, Charles A. *The Culture of Organs.* New York: P. B. Hoeber, 1938.

Foreword and map drawings to *Listen! The Wind,* by Anne M. Lindbergh. New York: Harcourt, Brace & Co., 1938.

"Appeal for Isolation." *Vital Speeches of the Day* (1 October 1939): 751–52.
Text of radio address from Washington, D.C., 15 September 1939.

"Aviation, Geography, and Race." *Reader's Digest* (November 1939): 64–67.

"What Our Decision Should Be." *Vital Speeches of the Day* (1 November 1939): 57–59.
Text of radio address from Washington, D.C., 13 October 1939.

"What Substitute for War?" *Atlantic Monthly* (March 1940): 304–308.
An abridgement appeared in *Reader's Digest* (May 1940): 43–47.

"Our National Safety." *Vital Speeches of the Day* (1 June 1940): 484–85.
Text of radio address, 19 May 1940.

"Our Drift toward War." *Vital Speeches of the Day* (1 July 1940): 549–51.
Text of radio address, 15 June 1940.

"Appeal for Peace." *Vital Speeches of the Day* (15 August 1940): 644–46.
Delivered at a Keep-America-Out-Of-War rally, Chicago, 4 August 1940.

"Plea for American Independence." *Scribner's Commentator* (December 1940): 69–73.

The Radio Addresses of Charles A. Lindbergh. New York: Scribner's Commentator, 1940.

"Impregnable America." *Scribner's Commentator* (January 1941): 3–6.

"Our Air Defense." *Vital Speeches of the Day* (1 February 1941): 241–42.
Delivered before the House Foreign Affairs Committee, 23 January 1941.

"We Are Not Prepared for War." *Vital Speeches of the Day* (15 February 1941): 266–67.
Delivered before the Senate Foreign Relations Committee, 6 February 1941.

"A Letter to Americans." *Collier's* (29 March 1941): 14, 75–77.

"We Cannot Win This War for England." *Vital Speeches of the Day* (1 May 1941): 424–26.
Delivered at an America First Committee meeting, Newark, 23 April 1941.

"Election Promises Should Be Kept." *Vital Speeches of the Day* (1 June 1941): 482–83.
Delivered at Madison Square Garden, 23 May 1941.

"Lindbergh for the Record: Views on the Great Controversial Issues of the Day." *Scribner's Commentator* (August 1941): 7–13.

"Who Are the War Agitators?" *Des Moines Register,* (12 September 1941) 6:1; and *Chicago Tribune* (12 September 1941) 1:6, 10:6–8.
Delivered at the Des Moines Coliseum, 11 September 1941.

"Time Lies with Us." *Scribner's Commentator* (November 1941): 88–93.

Of Flight and Life. New York: Charles Scribner's Sons, 1948.
An abridgement appeared in *Reader's Digest* (September 1948): 1–6, 133–38.

"A Lesson from the Wright Brothers." *Aviation Week* (26 December 1949): 42.
Acceptance speech made on receiving the 1949 Wright Brothers Memorial Trophy at the Aero Club of Washington, D.C., 17 December 1949, on the forty-sixth anniversary of the first powered flight. The article also appeared as "Human Qualities Must Keep Pace with Science," National Aeronautic Association, *National Aeronautics and Flight Plan* (January 1950): 6; and as "Man Cannot Thrive Indefinitely in the Hothouse Atmosphere We Are Creating," *U.S. Air Services* (January 1950): 11, 13.

Preface to *The Voyage to Lourdes,* by Alexis Carrel. Translated from the French by Virgilia Peterson. New York: Harper & Bros., 1950.

The Spirit of St. Louis. New York: Charles Scribner's Sons, 1953.
An abridgement appeared as "Thirty-three Hours to Paris," *Saturday Evening Post* (11 April–13 June 1953); and in *Reader's Digest* (October 1953): 143–80.

"I Have Stated a Problem — You Have the Right to Ask for a Solution." *U.S. Air Services* (March 1954): 17–19.
Address delivered at the Institute of Aeronautical Sciences Honors Night Dinner, New York, Hotel Astor, 25 January 1954, when Lindbergh was presented with the Daniel Guggenheim Medal for pioneering efforts in flight and aerial navigation. The address also appeared as "The Fourth Dimension of Survival," *Saturday Review* (22 February 1954): 11–12; and "The Future Character of Man," *Vital Speeches of the Day* (1 March 1954): 293–95.

"Our Best Chance to Survive." *Saturday Evening Post* (17 July 1954): 25.

"Thoughts of a Combat Pilot." *Saturday Evening Post* (2 October 1954): 20–21, 78, 80.

An abridgement appeared as "The Church in the Gunsight," *Reader's Digest* (December 1954): 11–14.

Preface to *This High Man: The Life of Robert H. Goddard,* by Milton Lehman. New York: Farrar, Straus & Co., 1963.

"Is Civilization Progress?" *Reader's Digest* (July 1964): 67–74.

Foreword to *Challenge to the Poles: Highlights of Arctic and Antarctic Aviation,* by John Grierson. Hamden Conn.: Archon Books, 1964.

"Wisdom of Wildness." *Life* (22 December 1967): 8–10.

"A Letter from Lindbergh." *Life* (4 July 1969): 60A–61.

The Wartime Journals of Charles A. Lindbergh. New York: Harcourt Brace Jovanovich, 1970.

Excerpts from the *Wartime Journals* appeared in *American Scholar* (Autumn 1970): 577–613; and in *American Heritage* (October 1970): 32–37, 114–15.

"Way of Wildness." *Reader's Digest* (November 1971): 90–93.

Foreword to *Vanguard: A History,* by Constance M. Green and Milton Lomask. Washington, D.C.: Smithsonian Institution Press, 1971.

Lindbergh discusses his contacts with the American satellite development program.

"Feel the Earth." *Reader's Digest* (July 1972): 62–65.

"For Me, Aviation Has Value Only to the Extent that It Contributes to the Quality of the Human Life It Serves." *New York Times,* 27 July 1972, 31: 2–4.

"Lessons from the Primitive." *Reader's Digest* (November 1972): 147–51.

Boyhood on the Upper Mississippi: A Reminiscent Letter. St. Paul: Minnesota Historical Society, 1972.

Foreword to *Lindbergh of Minnesota: A Political Biography,* by Bruce L. Larson. New York: Harcourt Brace Jovanovich, 1973.

"Some Remarks at the Dedication of Lindbergh State Park Interpretive Center." *Minnesota History* (Fall 1973): 275–76.

Foreword to *Carrying the Fire: An Astronaut's Journeys,* by Michael Collins. New York: Farrar, Straus & Giroux, 1974.

Foreword to *The Gentle Tasasday: A Stone-Age People in the Philippine Rain Forest,* by John Nance. New York: Harcourt Brace Jovanovich, 1975.

An Autobiography of Values. To be published by Harcourt Brace Jovanovich in 1978.

Biographical and Related Studies of Charles A. Lindbergh Books

Beamish, Richard J. *The Boy's Story of Lindbergh: The Lone Eagle.* Philadelphia: John C. Winston Co.,1928.
Also published in 1927 as *The Story of Lindbergh.*

Beauregard, Marie Antoinette, comp. *Illustrations of Colonel Lindbergh's Decorations and Some of His Trophies, Received within the Year Following His Transatlantic Flight of May 20–21, 1927.* St. Louis: Missouri Historical Society, 1928.

Bruno, Harry A. *Wings Over America: The Story of American Aviation.* Garden City, N. Y.: Halcyon House, 1944.
See chap. 11, "Young Lindbergh."

Burden, James H. *An Interpretation of Colonel Lindbergh's Achievements.* Sacramento: n.p., 1928.

Cole, Wayne S. *America First: The Battle against Intervention, 1940–1941.* Reprint ed. New York: Octagon Books, 1971.
Contains extensive material concerning Lindbergh's involvement in the America First Committee.

Cole, Wayne S. *Charles A. Lindbergh and the Battle against American Intervention in World War II.* New York: Harcourt Brace Jovanovich, 1974.
Includes a bibliography, pp. 279–84.

Condon, John F. *Jafsie Tells All! Revealing the Inside Story of the Lindbergh-Hauptmann Case.* New York: Jonathan Lee, 1936.

Davis, Kenneth S. *The Hero: Charles A. Lindbergh and the American Dream.* Garden City, N.Y.: Doubleday & Co.,1959.
Includes a long bibliographical essay, pp 434–515.

Delear, Frank J. *Igor Sikorsky: His Three Careers in Aviation.* New York: Dodd, Mead & Co., 1976.
Portions of this book detail Lindbergh's association with Igor Sikorsky.

Eubank, Nancy. *The Lindberghs: Three Generations.* St. Paul: Minnesota Historical Society, 1975.

Fife, George B. *Lindbergh, The Lone Eagle: His Life and Achievements.* New York: A. L. Burt Co., 1927.

Fraser, Chelsea. *Famous American Flyers.* New York: Thomas Y. Crowell Co., 1941.
See "Charles A. Lindbergh," pp. 151–79.

Gill, Brendan. *Lindbergh Alone.* New York: Harcourt Brace Jovanovich, 1977.
An abridgement appeared in *Reader's Digest* (May 1977): 255–86.

Grierson, John. *I Remember Lindbergh.* New York: Harcourt Brace Jovanovich, to be published in late 1977.

Guggenheim, Harry F. *The Seven Skies*. New York: G. P. Putnam's Sons, 1930.
See "The Significance of the Lindbergh Flight," pp. 73–91.

Haines, Lynn, and Haines, Dora B. *The Lindberghs*. New York: Vanguard Press, 1931.
Chiefly concerns Lindbergh's father, C. A. Lindbergh, and the Lindbergh family.

Hallion, Richard P., Jr. *Legacy of Flight: The Guggenheim Contribution to American Aviation*. Seattle: University of Washington Press, 1977.
Portions of *Legacy of Flight* deal with Lindbergh's association with The Daniel Guggenheim Fund for the Promotion of Aeronautics.

Haring, John V. *The Hand of Hauptmann*. Plainfield, N.J.: Hamer, 1937.

Keyhoe, Donald E. *Flying with Lindbergh*. New York: G. P. Putnam's Sons, 1928.
Concerns Lindbergh's forty-eight-state flying tour.

Lardner, John. "The Lindbergh Legends." In: *The Aspirin Age, 1919–1941*, pp. 190–213. Edited by Isabel Leighton. New York: Simon & Schuster, 1949.

Larson, Bruce L. *Lindbergh of Minnesota: A Political Biography*. Foreword by Charles A. Lindbergh, Jr. New York: Harcourt Brace Jovanovich, 1973.
Deals mainly with the airman's father.

Leipold, L. Edmond. *Charles A. Lindbergh, Aviation Pioneer*. Men of Achievement Series. Minneapolis: Denison and Co., 1972.

Lindbergh, Anne M. *Bring Me a Unicorn: Diaries and Letters of Anne Morrow Lindbergh, 1922–1928*. New York: Harcourt Brace Jovanovich, 1972.

Lindbergh, Anne M. *The Flower and the Nettle: Diaries and Letters of Anne Morrow Lindbergh, 1936–1939*. New York: Harcourt Brace Jovanovich, 1976.

Lindbergh, Anne M. *Hour of Gold, Hour of Lead: Diaries and Letters of Anne Morrow Lindbergh, 1929–1932*. New York: Harcourt Brace Jovanovich, 1973.

Lindbergh, Anne M. *Locked Rooms and Open Doors: Diaries and Letters of Anne Morrow Lindbergh, 1933–1935*. New York: Harcourt Brace Jovanovich, 1974.

Lindbergh, Anne M. *The Wave of the Future: A Confession of Faith*. New York: Harcourt Brace & Co., 1940.

Lomask, Milton. *Seed Money: The Guggenheim Story*. New York: Farrar, Straus & Giroux, 1964.
Includes an account of Lindbergh's association with The Daniel Guggenheim Fund for the Promotion of Aeronautics.

Miller, Francis T. *Lindbergh: His Story in Pictures*. New York: G. P. Putnam's Sons, 1929.

Mosley, Leonard. *Lindbergh: A Biography*. Garden City, N.Y.: Doubleday & Co., 1976.
Includes source notes, pp. 394–428.

Nicholson, Sir Harold. *Diaries and Letters: 1930–1939.* Edited by Nigel Nicholson. New York: Atheneum, 1966.
Segments of this book deal with Nicholson's association with the Lindberghs while he was writing the biography of Dwight Morrow, Anne Morrow Lindbergh's father.

Nicholson, Sir Harold. *Dwight Morrow.* New York: Harcourt Brace & Co., 1935.
This biography of Anne Morrow Lindbergh's father contains useful information concerning Charles A. Lindbergh.

O'Brien, Patrick J. *The Lindberghs: The Story of a Distinguished Family.* Philadelphia: International Press, 1935.
Deals with Charles and Anne Morrow Lindbergh.

Pudney, John. *Six Great Aviators.* London: Hamish Hamilton, 1955.
See "Charles Lindbergh, the American Hero," pp. 123–56.

Reeves, Earl. *Lindbergh Flies On! A Story of a Hero, and of the Pioneers, and "Empire Builders of the Air" Who Followed Him.* New York: Robert M. McBride & Co., 1930.

Ross, Walter S. *The Last Hero: Charles A. Lindbergh.* Rev. ed. New York: Harper & Row, 1976.
Includes bibliographic notes, pp. 375–91.

Scaduto, Anthony. *Scapegoat: The Lonesome Death of Bruno Richard Hauptmann.* New York: G. P. Putnam's Sons, 1976.

Shoenfeld, Dudley D. *The Crime and the Criminal: A Psychiatric Study of the Lindbergh Case.* New York: Covici-Friede, 1936.

New Haven, Conn. Yale University Sterling Memorial Library. Truman Smith, Air Intelligence Activities Office of the Military Attaché American Embassy, Berlin, Germany, August 1935–April 1939, with Special Reference to the Services of Colonel Charles A. Lindbergh, Air Corps (Res.).
Colonel Smith was U.S. military attaché and military attaché for air in the U.S. embassy, Berlin, from 1935 to 1939. His report is an unpublished memoir.

Teale, Edwin W. *The Book of Gliders.* New York: E. P. Dutton & Co., 1930.
See chap. 5, "Noted Glider Pilots," for a description of Lindbergh's gliding activities and of his association with William Hawley Bowlus.

U.S. Department of State. *The Flight of Captain Charles A. Lindbergh from New York to Paris, May 20–21, 1927, as Compiled from the Official Records of the Department of State.* Washington, D.C.: U.S. Government Printing Office, 1927.

Van Every, Dale, and Tracy, Morris De Haven. *Charles Lindbergh, His Life.* New York: D. Appleton & Co., 1927.

Van Kampen, Isaac. *Lindbergh: A Saga of Youth.* Boston: Stratford Co., 1928.

Vitray, Laura. *The Great Lindbergh Hullaballoo: An Unorthodox Account.* New York: William Faro, 1932.

Waller, George. *Kidnap: The Story of the Lindbergh Case.* New York: Dial Press, 1961.

Wecter, Dixon. *The Hero in America: A Chronicle of Hero Worship.* New York: Charles Scribner's Sons, 1941.
See chap. 16, "Gods from the Machine: Edison, Ford, Lindbergh," pp. 415–44.

West, James E. *The Lone Scout of the Sky: The Story of Charles A. Lindbergh.* Philadelphia: John C. Winston Co., 1928.
Published for the Boy Scouts of America.

Whipple, Sidney B. *The Lindbergh Crime.* New York: Blue Ribbon Books, 1935.

Whipple, Sidney B., ed. *The Trial of Bruno Richard Hauptmann.* Garden City, N.Y.: Doubleday, Doran & Co., 1937.
An account of the proceedings of the Lindbergh kidnap trial.

PERIODICAL AND NEWSPAPER ARTICLES

Allen, C. B. "The Facts about Lindbergh." *Saturday Evening Post* (28 December 1940): 12–13, 50–53.

Allen, C. B. "Lindbergh: Ambassador of Flight." *Aerospace International* (May–June 1967): 10–11.

Allen, Richard S. "The Lockheed Sirius." *American Aviation Historical Society Journal* (Winter 1965): 266–80.

Bent, Silas. "Lindbergh and the Press." *Outlook* (April 1932): 212–14, 240.

Bing, Richard J. "The Public Knew Lindbergh as a Pilot, but He Explored Science, Too." *Los Angeles Times,* 25 September 1974, 5: 1–4.
Concerns Lindbergh's association with Alexis Carrel.

Bowers, Peter M. "The Many Splendid Spirits of St. Louis." *Air Progress* (June 1967): 15–18, 70–72.

Bowman, Pierre. "The 'Lone Eagle's' Last Flight." *Reader's Digest* (December 1974): 255–58, 260.
Obituary article.

Bruno, Harry A., and Dutton, William S. "Lindbergh, the Famous Unknown." *Saturday Evening Post* (21 October 1933): 23, 36, 38, 40.

Bruno, Harry A. "Why Slim Flew to Paris." *Aerospace Historian* (autumn 1967): 144-45.

Butterfield, Roger. "Lindbergh: Stubborn Young Man of Strange Ideas Becomes a Leader of Wartime Opposition." *Life* (11 August 1941): 64–70, 73, 74–75.

Butz, J. S., Jr. "New York to Paris: How Lindbergh Did It." *Aerospace International* (May–June 1967): 21–22, 25–27.

Carter, Dustin W. "Reflections on 'Lindy'." *American Aviation Historical Society Journal* (spring 1977): 10–11.

"Charles Augustus Lindbergh." *Washington Post,* 27 August 1974, A18: 1–2.
An editorial written at the time of Lindbergh's death.

Collins, Michael. "Showing Lindbergh the Air and Space Museum." *Saturday Review* (16 April 1977): 30, 34.

"Colonel Lindbergh's Homecoming." *Aero Digest* (July 1927): 31–32, 34.

"Commemorating the Twenty-fifth Anniversary of Lindbergh's New York–Paris Flight." *Aero Digest* (May 1952): 17–86.
Includes Admiral DeWitt Clinton Ramsey's "It Made Aviation as Well as History," pp. 18–21; Lauren D. Lyman's "Operation Zero," pp. 22–25; George F. McLaughlin's "Ryan NY-P *Spirit of St. Louis,*" pp. 26–32, 34, 36, 38, 40; and Lynn S. Black's "The Lindbergh Story," pp. 42–44 ff.

Considine, Bob. "Aloha Lindy." *Air Line Pilot* (May 1977): 32–33.
Reprinted from a story Considine wrote in 1974.

Crawford, Kenneth. "Charles Augustus Lindbergh: A Life of Superlatives." *Washington Post,* 27 August 1974, C3: 1–8.

Davidson, David. "The Story of the Century." *American Heritage* (February 1976): 23–29, 93.
Concerns the Lindbergh kidnapping case.

Davidson, Jesse. "The Plane that Flew to Paris." *Model Airplane News* (June 1937): 4–7, 36–38.

Edwards, A. J. "The Plane Colonel Lindbergh Used." *Slipstream* (July 1927): 13–14.
On the Ryan NYP, *Spirit of St. Louis.*

Erskine, John. "Flight: Some Thoughts on the Solitary Voyage of a Certain Young Aviator." *Century Magazine* (September 1927): 513–18.

Evans, Raymond. "Lindbergh at the Capital." *Outlook* (22 June 1927): 243–45.

"Fame and Privacy." *Nation* (20 August 1930): 195–96.
Editorial concerning Lindbergh's relationship with the press.

"From the Files: Lindbergh's Historic Story Told by NAA Records." National Aeronautic Association, *National Aeronautics* (June 1937): 7–8, 34.

Gann, Ernest K. "Thirty-three Hours that Changed the World." *Saturday Review* (16 April 1977): 7–10.

"Going Back Time." *New York Times,* 9 April 1972, 5: 1–2.
Mentions Lindbergh's concern for the Tasaday, a Stone-Age civilization in the Philippines.

Gregory John S. "What's Wrong with Lindbergh?" *Outlook* (3 December 1930): 530–34.
A description of Lindbergh's encounters with the press.

Grierson, John. "Charles A. Lindbergh — A Pioneer Remembered." Royal Aeronautical Society, *Aerospace* (October 1975): 12–13.
Lindbergh Memorial Lecture sponsored by the Royal Aeronautical Society in association with the Royal Aero Club and the Guild of Air Pilots and Air Navigators, 21 May 1975, and delivered on the forty-eighth anniversary of the solo transatlantic flight. *See also* Grierson's "The Lindbergh Story," *Aeroplane Monthly* (February 1976): 66–72, and (March 1976): 161–66, for identical material.

Gurney, Harlan. "The Spirit of Lindbergh." *Air Line Pilot* (May 1977): 24–25.
Reprint of an article appearing in *Popular Aviation* (May–June 1967).

Hall, Donald A. "Special Facts and Figures on *Spirit of St. Louis.*" *Slipstream* (July 1927): 15.

Hall, Donald A. *Technical Note 257: Technical Preparation of the Airplane* Spirit of St. Louis. Washington, D.C.: National Advisory Committee for Aeronautics, July 1927.
See also his "Technical Preparation of the Ryan New York–Paris Airplane," *Aero Digest* (July 1927): 36, 38, 106.

Hallion, Richard P., Jr. "Charles Augustus Lindbergh." *Astronautics and Aeronautics* (October 1974): 65.
Obituary article.

"High Cost of Fame." *New Republic* (12 June 1929): 87–88.
An editorial on Lindbergh's dealings with the press.

Hinton, Walter. "What Lindbergh is Doing for Aviation." *Outlook* (22 June 1927): 246–49.

Horsfall, Jessie E. "Lindbergh's Start for Paris." *Aero Digest* (June 1927): 503–504, 506, 508.

Keasler, Jack. "The Search for Leon Klink." *American Aviation Historical Society Journal* (Summer 1976): 92–100.
Leon Klink was a friend of Lindbergh's during his barnstorming period.

Keasler, Jack. "Tracking the 'Lost' Barnstorming Pal of 'Slim' Lindbergh." *Smithsonian* (May 1976): 58–65.

Keller, Allan. "Over the Atlantic Alone: Charles Lindbergh's $25,000 Flight." *American History Illustrated* (April 1974): 38–45.

Ketchum, W. Q. "The Cruise of the Jelling: With Lindbergh into the North Atlantic." *Canadian Aviation* (January 1934): 7–9.

Keyhoe, Donald. "Lindbergh Four Years After." *Saturday Evening Post* (30 May 1931): 21, 46, 48, 53.

Keyhoe, Donald. "Seeing America with Lindbergh: The Record of a Tour of More than 20,000 Miles by Airplane through Forty-eight States on Schedule Time." *National Geographic Magazine* (January 1928): 1–46.

Larson, Bruce L. "Lindbergh's Return to Minnesota, 1927." *American Aviation Historical Society Journal* (spring 1977): 2–9.
Reprinted from *Minnesota History* (Winter 1970): 141–52.

Lehman, Milton. "How Lindbergh Gave a Lift to Rocketry." *Life* (4 October 1963): 115–18.

Lindbergh, Anne M. "Flying with Lindy." *New York Times,* 27 February 1972, sec. 4, 13: 3–4.

"Lindbergh Dies of Cancer in Hawaii at the Age of 72." *New York Times,* 27 August 1974, 1: 1–2.

"Lindbergh Ends Latin-American Tour." *Aero Digest* (March 1928): 340–41, 464–65.

"Lindbergh Inaugurates New Pan American Route." *Southern Aviation* (December 1931): 19.

"Lindbergh Names Two Key SST Defects: Warns of Sonic Boom and Upper Air Pollution." *New York Times,* 23 March 1971, 13:1.

"Lindbergh Opposes Further SST Work." *New York Times,* 6 February 1971, 59:4.

"Lindbergh Says Goddard Held Moon Shot Possible." *New York Times,* 24 May 1969, 16: 2–3.

"Lindbergh Says Technology, If Not Curbed, May Destroy Man." *New York Times,* 7 July 1970, 25: 1–5.

"The Lindbergh Survey." *U. S. Air Services* (January 1934): 10–13.

"Lindbergh's Central American Flight." *Aero Digest* (February 1928): 174, 301.

"Lindbergh's Flight to Mexico and Central America." *Aero Digest* (January 1928): 14–18.

"Lindbergh's Lockheed Seaplane." *Aero Digest* (July 1931): 60–64.
Concerns the Lindberghs' Lockheed Sirius, *Tingmissartoq,* used in their 1931 flight to the Orient and currently in the collection of the National Air and Space Museum, Smithsonian Institution.

"Lindbergh's Own Story of Epochal Flight." *New York Times,* 23 May 1927, 1: 5–8; 2: 1–4.
According to Walter S. Ross's *The Last Hero* (New York: Harper & Row, 1976, p. 139), the *Times'* story was ghostwritten for Lindbergh. *See also,* "My Flight to Paris," *Aero Digest* (June 1927): 514, 516, 518, 520, 524, and "Lindbergh's Own Story," New York Times Publication, *Current History* (July 1927): 513–22, for the syndicated account of the flight.

"Lindbergh's Survey Flight: The Equipment of the Lockheed 'Sirius'." *Flight* (1 March 1934): 187–88.

"Lindbergh's Take-off for Aviation." Aerospace Industries Association of America, *Aerospace* (December 1976): 14–16.

Loh, Jules. "Lindy, Yesterday's Famous Hero Is Today's Quiet Pioneer." Lansing, Michigan, *State Journal* (20 May 1962).

Lyman, Lauren D. "How Lindbergh Wrote a Book." United Aircraft Corporation, *Bee Hive* (Summer 1954): 18–20.
Tells how Lindbergh came to write *The Spirit of St. Louis.*

Lyman, Lauren D. "Lindbergh Family Sails for England to Seek a Safe, Secluded Residence." *New York Times,* 23 December 1931, 1:7–8; 3: 2–3.

Lyman, Lauren D. "The Lindbergh I Know." *Saturday Evening Post* (4 April 1953): 22–23, 84–88.

Lyman, Lauren D. "Lindbergh: 'Tech Rep.'" *National Air Review* (June 1950): 5–7.

Lyman, Lauren D. "Lindbergh's Flight — A Takeoff for Aviation." Aerospace Industries Association of America, *Aerospace* (May 1967): 2–5.
An excerpt from this article, "The Take-off," appeared in *Aerospace* (December 1976): 16.

Lyman, Lauren D. "When Lindbergh Went to Paris." United Aircraft Corporation, *Bee Hive* (Spring 1967): 15–21.

McFarland, Marvin W. "The Lindbergh Dinner." *U. S. Air Services* (February 1954): 17–18.
Concerns the Institute of the Aeronautical Sciences Honors Night Dinner held at the Hotel Astor in New York, 25 January 1954, at which Lindbergh made a rare public appearance.

McDonald, Charles. "Lindbergh in Battle." *Collier's* (16 February 1946): 11–12; and (23 February 1946): 26, 28, 30.
The author was commander of the 475th Fighter Group, U.S. Army Air Force, with which Lindbergh flew as a civilian advisor.

McLaughlin, George F. "The Ryan NYP Monoplane." *Aero Digest* (June 1927): 536–38.

Meier, F. C. "Collecting Microörganisms from the Arctic Atmosphere. With field notes and material by Charles A. Lindbergh." *Scientific Monthly* (January 1935): 5–20.

Mitchell, Henry. "Celebrating the Lonely Drama of Lucky Lindy's Flight." *Washington Post,* 20 May 1977, B1: 1–3; B2.

Morgan, Len. "Lindbergh Is Gone." *Flying* (November 1974): 60–63.
Obituary article.

Mott, T. Bentley. "Herrick and Lindbergh." *World's Work* (January 1930): 66–72.

Newton, Wesley P. "The Third Flight: Charles A. Lindbergh and Aviation Diplomacy in Latin America, 1927–1928." *American Aviation Historical Society Journal* (Summer 1975): 94–102.

Northrop, Marvin A. "Lindbergh, the Jenny Pilot." *Western Flying* (May 1937): 18–19.

Notice of the Award of the Langley Medal to Charles A. Lindbergh, *Science* (1 July 1927): 9.

Nute, Grace L. "The Lindbergh Colony." *Minnesota History* 20 (1939): 243–58.
Concerns the Lindbergh family and its ancestry.

Owen, Russell. "Lindbergh's 'Embassy of Good Will' to Mexico." *Literary Digest* (24 December 1927): 3–4.

Owen, Russell. "Lindbergh's Epoch-making Flight from New York to Paris." *Current History* (July 1927): 506–512; 608–610.

Pearson, Drew, and Allen, Robert S. "Why Lindbergh Came Home." *Popular Aviation* (October 1939): 10–11, 62.

Petrie, Valerie. "Lindbergh Transatlantic Flight: Forty-ninth Anniversary Retrospective." *Air Progress* (May 1976): 72–73.
Includes a color three-view drawing of the *Spirit of St. Louis*

"Pioneer Flier Advanced Medicine by Designing Organ Perfusion Pump." *Journal of the American Medical Association* (23 May 1977): 2270–71.

"Preliminary Plans of the New York–Paris Flight." *Slipstream* (July 1927): 9–13.

"President Coolidge Bestows Lindbergh Award: The National Geographic Society's Hubbard Medal Is Presented to Aviator before the Most Notable Gathering in the History of Washington." *National Geographic Magazine* (January 1928): 132–40.

"President Leads the Nation in Tribute to Lindbergh." *New York Times,* 27 August 1974, 17: 4–8.

Quigley, Walter E. "Like Father, Like Son." *Saturday Evening Post* (21 June 1941): 27, 34, 39–40, 42.

Roberts, Chalmers. "The Spirit of Lindbergh." *Washington Post,* 29 August 1974, A30: 3–5.

Rolfe, Douglas. "From the *Spirit* to Space." Ryan Aeronautical Co. *Ryan Reporter* (May–June 1967): 2–7.

Ross, Nancy. "The Man Lindbergh Didn't Forget." *Washington Post,* 29 June 1973, B2: 1–4.
Concerns Lindbergh's praise of Alexis Carrel in a speech given at Georgetown University Hospital in ceremonies marking the centennial of Carrel's birth.

Ross, Walter S. "Where Did Charles Lindbergh Go?" *Esquire* (October 1963): 85–88, 152, 154, 156, 159.

Roth, Myron A. "The Week that Congress Flew." *Air Line Pilot* (May 1977): 31. Recounts Lindbergh's airborne sightseeing tour for Washington dignitaries during a week in March 1928 and how it influenced Congressional interest in aviation.

Shearer, Lloyd. "The Great and Controversial Hero." *Parade* (13 March 1977): 1, 4–5, 7–9.

"Simple Service for Lindbergh Held at Tiny Church in Hawaii." *New York Times,* 29 August 1974, 34: 4–5.

"Some Technical Notes on Lindbergh's Lockheed." *Aero Digest* (February 1934): 46, 49.

Sondern, Frederic J. "Lindbergh Walks Alone." *Life* (3 April 1939): 64–75.

Strnad, Frank. "The Lindbergh Jenny Story." *American Aviation Historical Society Journal* (Winter 1975): 218–22.

Skardon, James A. and McVay, Roseanne. "Flight from Fame." *Coronet* (July 1957): 31–43.

Thompson, Craig. "Did They Really Solve the Lindbergh Case?" *Saturday Evening Post* (8 March 1952): 26–27, 65–66, 70, 73, 75–77, 79–80.

Tozer, Eliot. "Lindbergh's Amazing Airplane." *Popular Science* (May 1957): 56–59. On the Ryan NYP, *Spirit of St. Louis.*

Van Dusen, William I. "Charlie Lindbergh — Glider Pilot." *Western Flying* (May 1930): 50–53, 143.

Van Dusen, William I. "Exploring the Maya with Lindbergh." *Saturday Evening Post* (11 January 1930): 40, 43, 54, 157–58.

Vecsey, George. "First Lindbergh Aeroplane Taking Shape Again on Long Island." *New York Times,* 17 June, 1975, 35:1. Lindbergh's Curtiss Jenny.

Ward, John W. "The Meaning of Lindbergh's Flight." In: *Studies in American Culture: Dominant Ideas and Images,* pp. 27–40. Edited by Joseph J. Kwiat and Mary C. Turpie. Minneapolis: University of Minnesota Press, 1960. Also appeared in *American Quarterly* (Spring 1958): 3–16.

Warren, Lella. "Before the Flight." *Collier's* (18 July 1931): 18–19, 42–44.

Watter, Michael. "Engineering Aspects of Lindbergh's Transatlantic Flight." *Aero Digest* (October 1927): 396–97, 483–85.

Weems, P. V. H. "The Flight of the *Tingmissartoq:* The Authoritative Account of the 1933 Survey Flights of the Lindberghs." *Aviation* (February 1934): 33–36; (April 1934): 102–105.

Well, Martin. "Charles Lindbergh Dies of Cancer in Hawaii." *Washington Post,* 27 August 1974, A1:1.

Weyer, Edward M., Jr. "Exploring Cliff Dwellings with the Lindberghs." *World's Work* (December 1929): 52–57.

Wheeler, Curtis. "Lindbergh in New York." *Outlook* (22 June 1927): 245–46.

Whitman, Alden. "Anne Morrow Lindbergh Reminisces about Life with Lindy." *New York Times Magazine* (8 May 1977): 16–18, 22, 26, 30.

Whitman, Alden. "Daring Lindbergh Attained Unattainable with Historic Flight Across Atlantic." *New York Times,* 27 August 1974, 18: 1–6.
Written at the time of Lindbergh's death.

Whitman, Alden. "The Price of Fame." *New York Times Magazine* (8 May 1977): 12–15.

Whitman, Alden. "The Return of Charles Lindbergh." *New York Times Magazine* (23 May 1971): 28–29, 44, 46, 48–49, 59.

Wilford, John N. "Lindbergh Memorial Fund Begun by Doolittle and Armstrong." *New York Times,* 20 October 1976, 22: 2–3.

Witze, Claude. "The Man at Mankind's Elbow." *Aerospace International* (May–June 1967): 15–16, 18.

DOMINICK A. PISANO is the reference librarian at the National Air and Space Museum. After graduating from Pennsylvania State University in 1966, he was commissioned as an officer in the United States Air Force, where he held various positions in technical training and maintenance squadrons. He received his master's degree in library science from Catholic University in 1974.

Charles A. Lindbergh

The National Air and Space Museum is pleased to announce the establishment of the Charles A. Lindbergh Chair of Aerospace History. The chair will be offered, for a term of one or more years, to the foremost historians working in the fields of aviation or space history. By endowing a chair in Lindbergh's name, the museum hopes to keep the great aviator's memory alive at the Smithsonian, where his *Spirit of St. Louis* is on permanent display.

The first encumbent of the Lindbergh chair will be Charles Harvard Gibbs-Smith, Keeper Emeritus of the Victoria and Albert Museum in London. An internationally recognized historian of flight specializing in the early days, Gibbs-Smith was educated at Harvard University and has published extensively. His best-known book, *Aviation: An Historical Survey,* is considered a landmark in the field. Charles Harvard Gibbs-Smith will arrive at the museum in January 1978. In addition to continuing his research, he will assist in lecture and publishing programs.